New England

Covered Bridges

Harold Stiver

Copyright Statement

New England Covered Bridges

Copyright 2024 Harold Stiver

Version 2.0
ISBN # 9780986867071

Table of Contents

Massachusetts

New Hampshire

Orange County

Orleans County

Rutland County

Washington County

Windham County

Windsor County

Windsor County,VT and Sullivan County, NH

Tours

Indexes

How to use this Book

New England has 150 surviving Historical Covered Bridges. For each of these Covered Bridges we have included photographs as well as descriptive and statistical data. Traditional Covered Bridges are those that follow the building practices of the Nineteenth Century and the early part of the Twentieth Century or those built later that follow those methods. All of these bridges have had repairs done as portions wear out, and some may have been almost entirely replaced through the years. I have used "The National Society for the Preservation of Covered Bridges, Inc." list of what they consider as Traditional Bridges.

Following is data included for each bridge

Name: This is listed in bold type, and where there are other names, it is the common name or the name listed on an accompanying plaque.

Other Names: Underneath the Common Name in brackets, you will find other names that the bridge has been known by.

Township and **County** are listed.

GPS Position: Enter the coordinates in a good GPS unit and it should take you right there. You, of course, must use care that you are not led off road or on a dangerous route. In particular be careful you are not led onto a non-maintained road in the winter.

Builder: If known, the name of the original builder(s) is listed.

Year Built: As well as the year built, if it has been moved it will shown with the year preceded by the letter M and, if a major repair has been done, the year will be shown preceded by the letter R.

Truss Type: The type for the particular bridge will be listed. If you are interested in more information on the various types of trusses, access "Truss Types" from the Table of Contents.

Dimensions: The length and number of spans.

Photo Tips: We try to give you some idea of what opportunities you have as well as restrictions, and special items you may want to incorporate into the picture. You may also find some useful ideas from reading "Photographing Covered Bridges" from the Table of Contents.

Notes: A place where you can find additional items of interest about the bridge.

World Index Number:
Covered bridges are assigned a number to keep track of them which consists of three numbers separated by hyphens.
 The first number represents the number of the U.S. State in alphabetical order. Following number 50 for the 50th state are additional numbers for Canadian provinces. Thus the numbers 05 represents California.
The second set of numbers represents the county of that state, again based on alphabetical order. Humboldt is the 12th county alphabetically in California, and it is designated as 05-12.
Each bridge in that county is given a number as it was discovered or built. Zane's Ranch was the fifth bridge discovered or built in the County of Humboldt, California and it therefore has the designation of 05-12-05. Sometimes you will see the first set of numbers replaced by the abbreviation for the state, thus CA-12-05.
A bridge is sometimes substantially rebuilt or replaced and it then has the suffix #2 added to it.

National Register of Historic Places: If the bridge has been registered, the date is given.

Photographing Covered Bridges

Some standard positions

Portal: Taken to show the ends of bridge or bridge opening. This view, usually symmetrical, will include various signs posted. This is also a good way to get run over, so be careful!

3/4 view: Shows both the front and sides of the bridge, and is often the most attractive.

Side view: Taken from a bank or from the river, this gives not only a nice view of the bridge but usually allows for some interesting foreground elements.

Interior view: An image taken from the interior of the bridge will show some interesting structure but there is not a lot of available light. A tripod is important and HDR processing is helpful.

Landscape View: With the bridge smaller in the frame, you can introduce the habitat around it, particularly effective with colorful autumn foliage.

Using HDR(High Dynamic Range)

HDR is a process where multiple images of varying exposure are combined to make one image.

It has a bad name with some people because many HDR images are super-saturated, a kind of digital age version of an Elvis painted on velvet. However, the process is actually about getting a full range of exposure with no burnt out highlights or blocked shadows. This is an ideal processing solution for photographing Covered Bridges where you often have open light sky set against dark shadowed landscape and structure.

I use a series of three exposures at levels of -1 2/3, 0, +1 2/3, and this normally runs the full exposure range encountered. It is important to use a stable tripod.

One situation where you may need a larger series is shooting from within a bridge and using the window to frame an outside scene. The dynamic range is huge and you will need to have a series with a much larger range.

There are a number of software programs you can use to combine these images including newer editions of Photoshop. I use Photomatix which I have found very versatile and easy to use.

Best times for photographing bridges

Mornings and evenings are generally the best times for outdoor photography but the use of HDR processing makes it easier even in bright direct light. Although any season is good for bridge photography including the winter, fall foliage included in a scene can be spectacular.

A Short History of Covered Bridges

Let's deal with that often posed question; "Why were the bridges covered"

1. Crossing animals thought it was a barn and entered easily. I like this suggestion, it shows imagination. However, its not the answer although the original bridges normally had no windows and this is said to be because animals would not be spooked by the sight of the water.

2. To cover up the unsightly truss structure. I don't think those early pioneers were that sensitive, and personally, I like the look of the trusses.

3. To keep snow off the traveled portion. In fact the bridge owners often paid to have the insides "snowed" in order to facilitate sleighs.

4. It offered some privacy to courting couples, hence "kissing bridges". That is a nice romantic notion but no.

In fact, the bridge was covered for economic reasons. The truss system was where much of the bridge's cost was found, and if left open to the elements, it deteriorated and the bridge became unstable and unsafe. Covering it protected this valuable portion and the roof could be replaced as needed with inexpensive materials and unskilled labor.

Without coverings, a bridge might only have a life span of a decade while one that was covered often lasted 75 years or more before repairs became necessary. Besides extending the longevity of a bridge, wooden covered bridges had the virtue that they could be constructed of local materials and there were many available workers skilled in working with wood.

The first known Covered Bridge in North America was built in 1804 by Theodore Burr. It was called the Waterford bridge and it spanned the Hudson River in New York.

For the rest of the century and into the 20th Century, Covered bridge building boomed as the country became populated and people needed to travel between communities. The cost of constructing and maintaining a bridge was normally borne by the nearby community and many bridges charged a toll as a method of offsetting these costs.

The period from 1825 to 1875 was the heyday of bridge building but near the end of that period iron bridges began to supplant them.

The number of Covered bridges may have numbered 10,000 but have now dropped to about 840 spread throughout North America. Many have Historical Designations which provides them protection and many communities are interested in protecting their local historical bridges.

Connecticut County Map

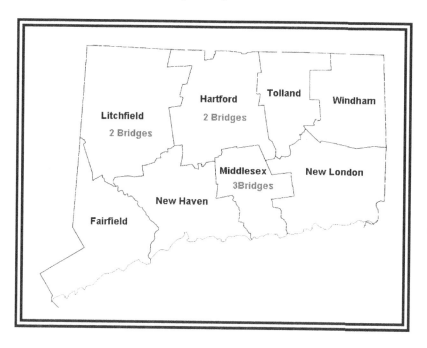

Bull's Covered Bridge
County: Litchfield, Connecticut
Township: Kent

GPS Position: N 41° 40.547' W 73° 30.537'
Directions: Bull's Bay Covered Bridge is less than a mile from the Connecticut-New York border. From the town of Kent, drive south on US-7 for about 3.8 miles and make a right onto Bulls Bridge Road. The bridge site is straight ahead.
Crosses: Housatonic River
Carries: Bulls Bridge Road
Builder: Not Known
Year Built: 1842 (R1903) (R1949) (R1969) (R1994)
Truss Type: Town, Queen and King
Dimensions: 1 Span, 109 Feet
Photo Tip: There are easy views of the portals but watch for traffic. You can also make your way to the side at river height for good views.
Notes: The bridge is named after Isaac and Jacob Bull who erected a grist mill and iron works here in the 1760. George Washington crossed the Housatonic River near this site in 1781.

World Index Number: CT/07-03-01
National Register of Historic Places: 1972

West Cornwall Covered Bridge (Hart)
County: Litchfield, Connecticut
Township: Cornwall

GPS Position: N 41° 52.303' W 73° 21.799'
Directions: The Bridge is on the Sharon-Goshen Turnpike/ CT-128 just east of the intersection of US-7
Crosses: Housatonic River
Carries: Sharon-Goshen Turnpike

Builder: Not Known
Year Built: 1864 (R1940s) (R1973)
Truss Type: Town and Queen
Dimensions: 2 Spans, 242 Feet

Photo Tip: There is a place to park near the west end and you can get good side views from the southwest. Portal views are available but watch out for traffic.
Notes: Extensive repairs were needed in the 1940s after a tanker truck plunged through the deck. Hidden steel supports were added in 1973

World Index Number: CT/07-03-02
National Register of Historic Places: 1972

Comstock Covered Bridge
County: Middlesex, Connecticut
Township: East Hampton

GPS Position: N 41° 33.188' W 72° 26.912'
Directions: From the town of Colchester, go west on Middlesex Rd./ CT-16 for 6 miles and turn right onto Bridge St. The bridge is a short distance.
Crosses: Salmon River
Carries: Bridge St. (Closed)
Builder: Not Known
Year Built: 2011 (Original 1873)
Truss Type: Howe
Dimensions: 1 Span, 94 Feet

Photo Tip: The bridge is in beautiful shape after the 2012 repairs. Side views are possible.
Notes: The 2012 repair was needed after a beer truck plunged through the deck. It is said that nearby residents recovered the beer. The fate of the driver is not mentioned. Steel reinforcing beams have been added under the current rebuild.

World Index Number: CT/07-04-01#2
National Register of Historic Places: January 1, 1976

Johnsonville Covered Bridge (Bicentennial)
County: Middlesex, Connecticut
Township: Moodus

GPS Position: N 41° 29.801' W 72° 27.669'
Directions: From the town of Moodus, go west on Moodus Leesville Rd/ CT-151 for less than a mile and turn left on Plains Rd and then left on Leesville Rd. The bridge is down in a valley on the north side of Leesville Rd.
Crosses: Moodus River
Carries: Private Road
Builder: Thomas Kronenberger
Year Built: 1976
Truss Type: Multiple Kingpost and Burr Arch
Dimensions: 1 Span, 60 Feet
Photo Tip: The Bridge is on private property and access is no longer being granted. It is possible to get telephoto images from Leesville Rd.
Notes: The bridge was built as a centennial project by bridgebuilder, Thomas Kronenberger. It is a shame that it cannot be examined in detail as it is an impressive structure which includes a pedestrian walkway.

World Index Number: CT/07-04-07
National Register of Historic Places: Not listed

Comstock Pony Truss Extension
County: Middlesex, Connecticut
Township: East Hampton

GPS Position: N 41° 33.188' W 72° 26.912'
Directions: From the town of Colchester, go west on Middlesex Rd./ CT-16 for 6 miles and turn right onto Bridge St. The bridge is a short distance.

Crosses: Salmon River
Carries: Bridge St. (Closed)

Builder: Not Known
Year Built: 2011
Truss Type: Pony Queen
Dimensions: 1 Span, 36 Feet

Photo Tip: The entire approach can be included in images with a portal view.
Notes: As the "World Guide to Covered Bridges" includes bridges or approaches when the trusses are covered, we have included them as well.

World Index Number: CT/07-04-P01#2
National Register of Historic Places: Not listed

Gold Mine Covered Bridge
County: New London, Connecticut
Township: Norwich

GPS Position: N 41° 31.159' W 72° 07.629'
Directions: From the town of Norwich, CT, go east on the Salem Turnpike CT/82 and turn right/north onto Wawecus Hill Rd. You will find the bridge in a valley on the right side by 128 Wawecus Hill Rd.
Crosses: Pond
Carries: Pedestrian walk

Builder: Arnold M. Graton Associates
Year Built: 2015
Truss Type: Town
Dimensions: 1 Span, 60 Feet

Photo Tip: The side view is spectacular in autumn
Notes: The structure was built in the historic manner and moved into position by oxen.

World Index Number: CT/07-06-21
National Register of Historic Places: Not listed

Worthington Pond Farms Covered Bridge
County: Tolland, Connecticut
Township: Somers

GPS Position: N 42° 01.012' W 72° 24.810'
Directions: From the town of Somers, go east on Main St./ CT-190 for 1.2 miles and turn left on Turnpike Rd. After 0.8 miles turn right on Mountain Rd. and you will find the entrance to Worthington Farms on the right after 1.5 miles.

Crosses: Pond
Carries: Private Road

Builder: Ron Oullette
Year Built: 2002
Truss Type: Town
Dimensions: 1 Span, 61 Feet

Photo Tip: Easy from all sides
Notes: An interesting destination for a family outing. The bridge is quite substantial.

World Index Number: CT/07-07-92
National Register of Historic Places: Not listed

The Barn Yard Covered Bridge
County: Tolland, Connecticut
Township: Avon

GPS Position: N 41° 53.109' W 72° 27.888'
Directions: From the town of Rockville go north on CT-83 N/West Rd. from Union St. After 1.2 miles, you will find the bridge by on your left

Crosses: Belding Brook
Carries: Pedestrian walk

Builder: Great Country Timber Frames
Year Built: 2021
Truss Type: Town
Dimensions: 1 Span, 56 Feet

Photo Tip: Easy from all sides with some nice foreground elements
Notes: Built by local company in the historical manner

World Index Number: CT-07/07/09
National Register of Historic Places: Not listed

Connecticut Tour

8 Bridges - 4 hours 15 minutes driving

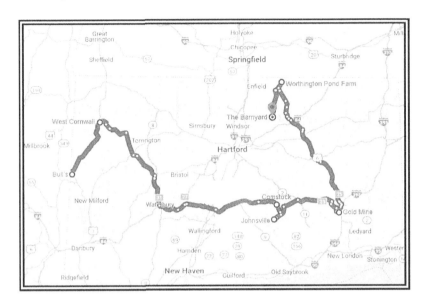

Bull's Covered Bridge	N 41° 40.547' W 73° 30.537'
West Cornwall CB	N 41° 52.303' W 73° 21.799'
Comstock and Pony	N 41° 33.188' W 72° 26.912'
Johnsonville Covered Bridge	N 41° 29.801' W 72° 27.669'
Gold MIne Covered Bridge	N 41° 31.159' W 72° 07.629'
Worthington Pond Farm CB	N 42° 01.012' W 72° 24.810'
The Barnyard Covered Bridge	N 41° 53.109' W 72° 27.888'

Maine County Map

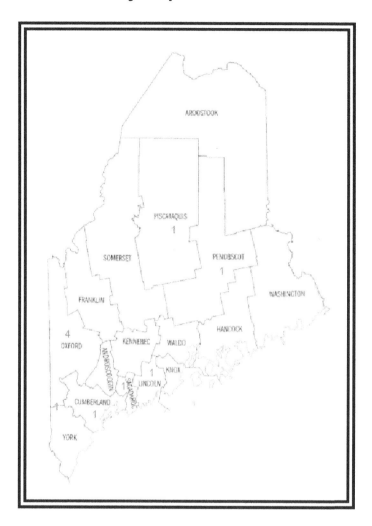

Babb's Covered Bridge
County: Cumberland, Maine
Township: Gorham-Windham

GPS Position: N 38° 19.450' W 84° 12.184'
Directions: From Windham go northwest on Roosevelt Trail for 1.0 mile and turn left on Page Rd. After 0.3 miles turn left on River Rd and drive 3.9 mi where you make a right on Covered Bridge Rd. The bridge is 0.4 miles along this road.
Crosses: Presumpscot River
Carries: Covered Bridge Road
Builder: Not known
Year Built: 1976 (Replaced an 1864 Bridge)
Truss Type: Queen
Dimensions: 1 Span, 79 feet
Photo Tip: There is a good river level side view accessible from the southeast
Notes: The original bridge was destroyed by fire on May 6, 1973, probably due to arson. It was rebuilt and the new bridge, which is an exact replica of the original, was completed on July 4, 1976. It was also built using the original techniques.

World Index Number: ME/19-03-01#2
National Register of Historic Places: Not listed

Trout Brook Covered Bridge (White)
County: Lincoln, Maine
Township: Alna

GPS Position: N 44° 06.311' W 69° 37.077'
Directions: From Alna, go southwest on Dock Rd for 0.7 miles and turn left on ME-218. After 0.4 miles you will find the WW & F Railway right of way near Peaslee Rd. The bridge is 0.2 mi west on the right of way

Crosses: Trout Brook
Carries: Wiscasset, Waterville & Farmington Railway right of way

Builder: Barns and Bridges of New England .
Year Built: 2018
Truss Type: Boxed Pony Howe
Dimensions: 1 Span, 47 feet

Notes: This is a recent addition to the Maine Covered Bridge List. The current bridge is based on a 1918 structure situated in New Hampshire. Metal parts of the Howe Truss from the original were used with new timbers

World Index Number: ME/19-08-P06
National Register of Historic Places: Not listed

Lovejoy Covered Bridge (South Andover)
County: Oxford, Maine
Township: Andover

GPS Position: N 44° 35.607' W 70° 44.035'
Directions: From the town of Andover go south on ME-5/Main St for 2.8 miles and turn left on Covered Bridge Road where the bridge is 0.7 miles.

Crosses: Ellis River
Carries: Covered Bridge Road

Builder: Unknown
Year Built: 1867 (R1983)
Truss Type: Paddleford
Dimensions: 1 Span, 80 feet

Photo Tip: Good from front and sides and particularly nice views from river level
Notes: The unpainted sides are nicely weathered and the portals are white with red trim. The bridge was repaired and reinforced in 1983 after a truck plunged through the floor.

World Index Number: ME/19-09-01
National Register of Historic Places: February 16, 1970

Hemlock Covered Bridge
County: Oxford, Maine
Township: Fryeburg

GPS Position: N 44° 04.779' W 70° 54.151'
Directions: From the town of Fryeberg go north on ME-5/Main St for 6.6 mi and turn right on Frog Alley. After 0.9 mi turn left on Frog Alley/Hemlock Bridge Rd and the bridge is 1.1 miles.
Crosses: Old Course Saco River
Carries: Frog Alley/Hemlock Bridge Road

Builder: J. Berry
Year Built: 1857 (R1988)
Truss Type: Paddleford and Arch
Dimensions: 1 Span, 130 feet

Photo Tip: Great river level side view from the SE including a nice reflection
Notes: A beautiful structure with unpainted weathered sides complemented by a nice balance of small windows. The laminated burr arch was added to the Paddleford truss system at a later date as were steel reinforcing beams.

World Index Number: ME/19-09-02
National Register of Historic Places: February 16, 1970

Bennett-Bean Covered Bridge
County: Oxford, Maine
Township: Lincoln Plantation

GPS Position: N 44° 55.150' W 71° 02.264'
Directions: From the village of Wilsons Mills go south on ME-16?Wilsons Mills Rd for 0.7 miles and turn right on Littlehale Rd where the bridge is 0.3 miles. Note that Littlehale Road may be closed in winter
Crosses: Magalloway River
Carries: Littlehale Road

Builder: Mason brothers
Year Built: 1898 (R2005)
Truss Type: Paddleford
Dimensions: 1 Span, 100 feet

Photo Tip: Excellent 3/4 view shows off the partially open sides.
Notes: Although it was built in 1898, it was not covered until 1899. The bridge is closed to vehicle traffic. It is unpainted and nicely weathered

World Index Number: ME/19-09-03
National Register of Historic Places: February 16, 1970

Sunday River Covered Bridge (Artist)
County: Oxford, Maine
Township: Newry

GPS Position: N 44° 29.521' W 70° 50.591'
Directions: From Bethel go northwest on ME-26/ME-5/Us-2/Mayville Rd for 2.0 miles and turn left on Sunday River Road. The bridge is found in 3.8 miles.
Crosses: Sunday River
Carries: Sunday River Road

Builder: Nahum Mason
Year Built: 1872 (R2003)
Truss Type: Paddleford
Dimensions: 1 Span, 99 feet

Photo Tip: A photographer's favorite, the open sides provide light and the unpainted textured wood shows off its balanced lines.
Notes: The artist, John Enneking used this bridge for his subject on many occasions which gave rise to its alternate name.

World Index Number: ME/19-09-04
National Register of Historic Places: February 16, 1970

Porter-Parsonfield Covered Bridge
County: Oxford and York Counties, Maine
Township: Porter-Parsonfield

GPS Position: N 43° 47.437' W 70° 56.292'
Directions: From the town of Porter go south on ME-160/Ossipee Trail for 0.1 mile and turn left on ME-160/N Road and you will see the bridge in 0.3 miles
Crosses: Ossipee River
Carries: ME-160/N Road

Builder: J. Berry
Year Built: 1876 (R1999)
Truss Type: Paddleford
Dimensions: 2 Spans, 160 feet

Photo Tip: There is a wonderful wide side view from the new bridge but watch out for traffic.
Notes: The bridge was bypassed in 1960 but has been maintained in good shape by the towns of Porter and Parsonfield. The interior has suffered from graffiti, the scourge of many of these historic structures

World Index Number: ME/19-09-05 and ME/19-16-01
National Register of Historic Places: February 16, 1970

Robyville Covered Bridge
County: Penobscot, Maine
Township: Corinth

GPS Position: N 44° 56.572' W 68° 58.103'
Directions: From the town of Kenduskeag go northwest on Stetson Road for 0.7 miles and turn right on Line Road/Mudgett Road and continue for 1.8 miles. Turn right onto Black Road and after 0.3 miles go right on Covered Bridge Road and you will find the bridge in 0.2 miles
Crosses: Kenduskeag Stream
Carries: Covered Bridge Road
Builder: Royal A. Sweet
Year Built: 1872 (R1984)
Truss Type: Long
Dimensions: 1 Span, 97 feet

Photo Tip: There are good shots from all sides including water level side views from the west.
Notes: This windowless bridge is shingled front and sides and looks great in a quiet rural setting. It is still carrying vehicle traffic and at some point was reinforced with steel beams.

World Index Number: ME/19-10-02
National Register of Historic Places: February 16, 1970

Low's Covered Bridge
County: Guilford-Sangerville, Maine
Township: Piscataquis

GPS Position: N 45° 10.518' W 69° 18.849'
Directions: From the town of Gilford go east on ME-15/ME-16/Water St for 3.2 miles and turn right on Lowe's Bridge Road where you will see the bridge
Crosses: Piscataquis River
Carries: Lowe's Bridge Road

Builder: Unknown
Year Built: 1990 (Original bridge was built in 1857)
Truss Type: Long
Dimensions: 1 Span, 146 feet

Photo Tip: There are very good side and 3/4 views from the picnic table area
Notes: This bridge was built in an authentic manner to replace the original lost to a flood in 1987. The abutments have been raised to protect it from future floods. It is a great spot for a family picnic.

World Index Number: ME/19-11-01#2
National Register of Historic Places: Not listed

New Portland Wire Covered Bridge
County: Somerset, Maine
Township: New Portland

GPS Position: N 44° 53.427 W 70 05.602'
Directions: From the town of New Portland go north on Old Kingfield Road from the intersection of ME-146/River Road and shortly turn right on Wire Bridge Road. After 1.2 miles you will reach the bridge.
Crosses: Carrabassett River
Carries: Wire Bridge Road
Builder: David Elder and Captain Charles B. Clark
Year Built: 1866 (R1961)
Truss Type: (Suspension)
Dimensions: 1 Span, 198 feet

Photo Tip: There are easy shots from all sides including river level side views. Look also for an image that shows the far pier through the close one.
Notes: Listed in the "World Guide to Covered Bridges" and it is certainly an interesting structure. The bridge itself is not covered but the suspension towers are.

World Index Number: ME/19-13-S1
National Register of Historic Places: January 12, 1970

Maine Tour

5 Bridges- 3 hours driving

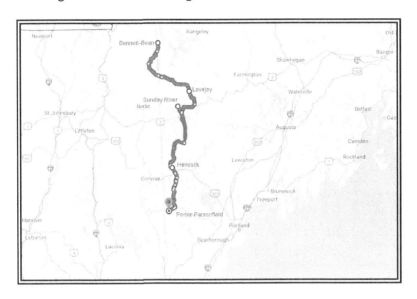

Bennet-Bean CB	N 44° 55.150' W 71° 02.264'
Lovejoy CB	N 44° 35.607' W 70° 44.035'
Sunday River CB	N 44° 29.521' W 70° 50.591'
Hemlock CB	N 44° 04.779' W 70° 54.151'
Porter-Parsonfield CB	N 43° 47.437' W 70° 56.292'

Massachusetts County Map

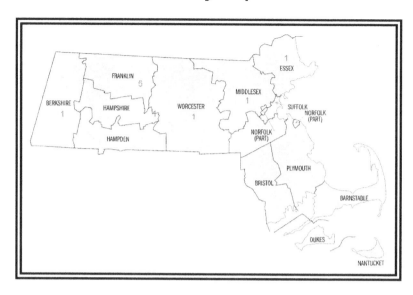

Upper Sheffield Covered Bridge
County: Berkshire, Massachusetts
Township: Sheffield

GPS Position: N 42° 07.428' W 73° 21.291'
Directions: From the town of Sheffield, turn east off of U.S.-7 onto Covered Bridge Lane near the north end of town and the bridge is a short distance

Crosses: Housatonic River
Carries: Covered Bridge Lane (Closed to vehicles)

Builder: Not known
Year Built: 1998 (Replaces one built in 1854)
Truss Type: Town
Dimensions: 1 Span, 93 feet

Photo Tip: It is easy to photograph from all sides
Notes: The original bridge was built in 1854 and was closed to vehicular traffic in 1976. It was destroyed by arson on Aug. 13, 1994 and was replaced in an historically authentic manner in 1998

World Index Number: MA/21-02-01#2
National Register of Historic Places: Not listed

Sawyer Pond Covered Bridge
County: Essex, Massachusetts
Township: Gloucester

GPS Position: N42° 35.477' W70° 43.129'
Directions: Take Western Ave/ Ma-127 northwest from Gloucester and go right on Magnolia Ave after about 3 miles. After 0.5 miles, you will be at the site
Crosses: Sawyer Pond
Carries: Private road

Builder: Frank Sawyer
Year Built: 1983
Truss Type: Town
Dimensions: 1 Span, 36 feet

Photo Tip: Although the bridge is on private property, it is easy to photograph one portal and the sides from the public roadway
Notes: It was built by Frank Sawyer from his age 73 to 76. It is presently used as storage for vehicles

World Index Number: MA/21-05-13
National Register of Historic Places: Not listed

Burkeville Covered Bridge (Conway)
County: Franklin, Massachusetts
Township: Conway

GPS Position: N 42° 30.450' W 72° 42.676'
Directions: Found at the west end of the town of Conway off MA-116 by Poland Rd.
Crosses: South River
Carries: Closed to Traffic

Builder: Not Known
Year Built: 1870 (Rebuilt 1999)
Truss Type: Howe
Dimensions: 1 Span, 106 feet

Photo Tip: There are easy side views for this bridge
Notes: This is often called the oldest surviving bridge in North America which it certainly is not. Hyde Hall in New York dates from 1825, and there are many other bridges which are built before 1870 which survive. It has been rebuilt a number of times and is presently in excellent shape.

World Index Number: MA/21-06-01
National Register of Historic Places: September 1, 1988

Pumping Station Covered Bridge (Williams)
County: Franklin, Massachusetts
Township: Greenfield

GPS Position: N:42° 38.789' W:72° 37.218'
Directions: Take exit 26 for MA-2 W toward Massachusetts 2A E/Greenfield Ctr/N Adams and at the roundabout, take the 1st exit onto MA-2 W/Mohawk Trail. Turn right onto Colrain Rd and after 1.6 miles, a slight right onto Plain Rd. Continue onto S Green River Rd. and a slight right onto Eunice Williams Dr. The bridge is at the end of the road
Crosses: Green River
Carries: Eunice Williams Dr (Closed to traffic at bridge)
Builder: J. Berry
Year Built: 1972 (R1988)
Truss Type: Paddleford and Arch
Dimensions: 1 Span, 130 feet

Photo Tip: Good from all sides. You can cross to the other side of the river for good views
Notes: It has received extensive repairs after damage from Hurricane Irene.

World Index Number: MA/21-06-02#2
National Register of Historic Places: Not listed

Arthur Smith Covered Bridge
County: Franklin, Massachusetts
Township: Colrain

GPS Position: N42° 40.184' W72° 43.074
Directions: From the Village of Colrain, take MA-112 west and you will find the bridge to the right on Lyonsville Rd
Crosses: North River
Carries: Lyonsville Rd

Builder: Not Known
Year Built: 2006 (The original bridge was built in 1870)
Truss Type: Burr Arch
Dimensions: 1 Span, 98 feet

Photo Tip: Easy to photograph from all angles including the sides at river level
Notes: There was a 1951 bridge that deteriorated in a nearby field for many years. The present structure may have used some of this bridge. It received minor damage from Hurricane Irene.

World Index Number: MA/21-06-03#2
National Register of Historic Places: Not listed

Bissell Covered Bridge
County: Franklin, Massachusetts
Township: Charlemont

GPS Position: N42° 37.898' W72° 52.133'
Directions: From the village of Claremont go north off MA-2/Mohawk Trail onto North Heath Rd. The bridge is about 0.3 miles.
Crosses: Mill Brook
Carries: North Heath Rd.
Builder: T.J. Harvey and Sons
Year Built: 1951
Truss Type: Long Variation
Dimensions: 1 Span, 92 feet

Photo Tip: Both upstream sides are easy to set up on and there is a dam just above the bridge which is interesting..
Notes: The original bridge at this site was built around 1882 and was used until the 1940s when it was closed as unsafe. A replacement was built in 1951. In 2003 the state planned on replacing it with a steel bridge but pressure from the citizens of Charlemont saved it

World Index Number: MA?21-06-04#2
National Register of Historic Places: Not listed

Creamery Covered Bridge
County: Franklin, Massachusetts
Township: Ashfield

GPS Position: N 42° 31.212' W 72° 48.384'
Directions: From the town of Ashfield, go west on MA-116 and and turn left on Ma-112/MA-116. The bridge is about 0.4 miles on the left
Crosses: Creamery Brook
Carries: Private Driveway

Builder: Dwight Scott
Year Built: 1985
Truss Type: Modified Queenpost
Dimensions: 1 Span, 40 feet

Photo Tip: The bridge is on private property, but you can photograph it from the public road
Notes: The bridge is on private property and is the entrance to their driveway. It was built by the owner in 1985

World Index Number: MA/21-06-11
National Register of Historic Places: Not listed

Gilbertsville-Ware Covered Bridge (Bridge Street)
County: Hampshire County and Worchester, MA
Township: Hardwick and Ware

GPS Position: N 42° 18.614' W 72° 12.737'
Directions: From Highway MA-32/Main St. in Gilbertview, Bridge St. crosses the Ware River and the bridge
Crosses: Ware River
Carries: Bridge St.
Builder: Richard Hawkins
Year Built: 1886 (Rebuilt 1986)
Truss Type: Town
Dimensions: 1 Span, 137 feet
Photo Tip: Pull off to park at the west end and you will find excellent set up positions from all sides. The southwest corner is especially good
Notes: The bridge was originally built in 1866 by the Boston and Maine Railroad Company when they took over an existing road for their tracks. In the early 1950s, plans were made to abandon the bridge but the towns on both sides of the river protested and repairs were made from 1956-1959. A major restoration was completed on its 100 year anniversary in 1986

World Index Number: MA/21-14-01
National Register of Historic Places: May 8, 1986

Pepperell Covered Bridge (Groton Street)
County: Middlesex, Massachusetts
Township: Pepperell

GPS Position: N 42° 40.177' W71° 34.505'
Directions: From the town of Pepperell take HollisSt/ MA-111 NW and turn right on Groton Rd. The Bridge is about 0.4 mile.
Crosses: Nashua River
Carries: Groton Rd
Builder: Various governments
Year Built: 2010
Truss Type: Pratt Variation
Dimensions: 1 Span, 108 feet

Photo Tip: Now that the new bridge is open, there are excellent views frpm all sides.
Notes: This is the third bridge at this site, recently completed after almost 2 years of construction. The original covered bridge was known as Nehemiah Jewett's Bridge. It was built in 1818 and replaced an uncovered bridge built in 1742.The second covered bridge on the site was known as Chester H. Waterous Covered Bridge and was built in 1963.

World Index Number: MA/21-09-01#3
National Register of Historic Places: Not listed

Vermont Covered Bridge (Dummerston, Taft)
County: Worchester, Massachusetts
Township: Sturbridge

GPS Position: N42° 06.348' W72° 05.726'
Directions: From Sturbridge, take Ma-131/ Main St. west and turn left on US-20. After 0.3 miles take a slight right onto Burgess School Rd and continue onto Old Sturbridge Village Rd. and continue to the parking area for the Old Sturbridge Village.
Crosses: Trib. of Quinebaug River
Carries: Private roadway
Builder: Not known
Year Built: 1874
Truss Type: Town
Dimensions: 1 Span, 55 feet
Photo Tip: Easy to photograph from all sides. Look for other interesting exhibit buildings in the area including a sawmill. There is also another covered bridge on a service road that starts across from the mill.
Notes: Originally situated in Dummerston, Vermont, it was moved to Old Sturbridge Village in 1952

World Index Number: MA/21-14-03
National Register of Historic Places: Not listed

Massachusetts Tour

Franklin County (5 Bridges-1hour 15 minutes driving)

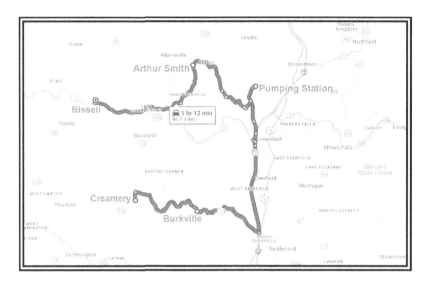

Creamery Covered Bridge   N 42° 31.212′ W 72° 48.384′
Burkville Covered Bridge   N 42° 30.450′ W 72° 42.676′
Pumping Station CB   N 42° 38.789′ W 72° 37.218′
Arthur Smith Covered Bridge   N 42° 40.184′ W 72° 43.074′
Bissell Covered Bridge   N 42° 37.898′ W 72° 52.133′

New Hampshire County Map

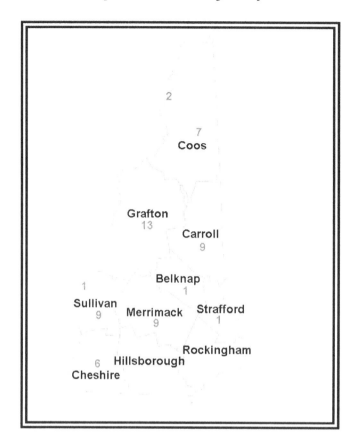

2

7
Coos

Grafton
13
Carroll
9

Belknap
1

1
Sullivan
9
Merrimack
9
Strafford
1

Rockingham

6 Hillsborough
Cheshire

Tannery Hill Covered Bridge
County: Belknap, New Hampshire
Township: Gilford

GPS Position: N 43° 32.980 W071° 24.321'
Directions: 47 Cherry Valley Rd, Gilford
Crosses: Gumstock River
Carries: None

Builder: Tim Andrews
Year Built: 1995
Truss Type: Town
Dimensions: 1 Span, 42 feet

Photo Tips: This bridge is on municipal property and the best view is of the portal
Notes: The bridge was built using local materials and is for pedestrian use only. It was built by the Rotary Club as a gift to the community of Guilford.

World Index Number: NH/29-01-03
National Register of Historic Places: Not listed

Jackson Covered Bridge (Honeymoon)
County: Carroll, New Hampshire
Township: Jackson

GPS Position: N 44° 08.499' W 71° 11.208'
Directions: From the town of Jackson, head southeast on NH-16 S for 0.4 mi and find the bridge
Crosses: Ellis River
Carries: NH16A

Builder: Charles Austin Broughton and son Frank Broughton
Year Built: 1876 (R1930) (R2004)
Truss Type: Paddleford and Arch
Dimensions: 1 Span, 121 feet

Photo Tips: There is not a good side view but the 3/4 view is excellent.
Notes: There is a tradition of newlyweds having their photos taken in the bridge which gives it its alternate name. The pedestrian walkway was added in the 1930 renovation.

World Index Number: NH/29-02-01
National Register of Historic Places: Not listed

Bartlett Covered Bridge
County: Carroll, New Hampshire
Township: Bartlett

GPS Position: N 44° 05.707 W 71° 12.211'
Directions: From the town of Bartlett, head east on US-302 E for 1.8 mi to see the bridge
Crosses: Saco River
Carries: Covered Bridge Lane

Builder: Unknown
Year Built: 1851 (R1966) (R1990)
Truss Type: Paddleford and Arch
Dimensions: 1 Span, 166 feet

Photo Tip: There is a good side view from the new bridge but be careful of traffic.
Notes: The building is presently a gift shop and there seems no problem in taking images of the bridge. Milton Graton did the renovations in 1966. The gift shop owners also operate the B&B next door.

World Index Number: NH/29-02-02
National Register of Historic Places: Not Listed

Saco River Covered Bridge
County: Carroll, New Hampshire
Township: Conway

GPS Position: N 43° 58.992' W 71° 07.019'
Directions: From the town of Bartlett, head north on Washington St for 0.2 mi and continue onto East Side Rd to find the bridge
Crosses: Saco River
Carries: East Side Rd
Builder: Charles Broughton and his son Frank Broughton
Year Built: 1890 (R1988)
Truss Type: Paddleford and Arch
Dimensions: 2 Span, 225 feet

Photo Tips: Good from all sides and a good river level side view from the south side.
Notes: This is the third covered bridge on this site. The first built in 1850 was destroyed when the Swift River Bridge crashed into it in a 1869 flood. The second was destroyed in an 1890 fire.

World Index Number: NH/29-02-03#3
National Register of Historic Places: Not listed

Swift River Covered Bridge
County: Carroll, New Hampshire
Township: Conway

GPS Position: N 43° 59.066' W 71° 07.175'
Directions: From Conway, head north on Washington St for 0.2 mi and take a slight left onto Washington St/West Side Rd and the bridge is 0.2 mi
Crosses: Swift River
Carries: Bypassed section of West Side Road

Builder: Jacob Berry and his son Jacob Berry Jr.
Year Built: 1890
Truss Type: Burr Arch
Dimensions: 1 Span, 97 feet

Photo Tips: Easy from all sides. Look for a nice side view from the new bridge but watch for traffic.
Notes: The present bridge replaced one swept away in a 1869 flood. The Paddleford trusses have had a burr arch added at some point

World Index Number: NH/29-02-05#2
National Register of Historic Places: Not listed

Albany Covered Bridge
County: Carroll, New Hampshire
Township: Albany

GPS Position: N 44° 00.342' W 71° 14.473'
Directions: From Conway, head NW on NH-112 W for 6.2 mi and turn right onto Passaconaway Rd and the bridge
Crosses: Swift River
Carries: Campground entrance road.

Builder: Amzi Russell and Leandre Morton
Year Built: 1858 (R1982)
Truss Type: Paddleford and Arch
Dimensions: 1 Span, 120 feet

Photo Tips: Easy from all sides including excellent side views.
Notes: Located in the White Mountain National Forest, there is a $5 admission charge. The open sides, unpainted textured sides and red roof make this a very picturesque bridge.

World Index Number: NH/29-02-06
National Register of Historic Places: Not listed

Durgin Covered Bridge
County: Carroll, New Hampshire
Township: Sandwich

GPS Position: N 43° 51.340' W 71° 21.866'
Directions: From the village of North Sandwich, head NW on Fellows Hill Rd for 1.4 mi and continue onto Foss Flats Rd and the bridge
Crosses: Cold River
Carries: Durgin Bridge Road

Builder: Jacob Berry
Year Built: 1869 (R1968) (R1983)
Truss Type: Paddleford and Arch
Dimensions: 1 Span, 96 feet

Photo Tips: Easy creek level side shots. The Paddleford and Arch system makes a nice image as well.
Notes: The 1968 renovation was done by Milton Graton and his son Arnold. The unpainted textured wood looks especially good in this natural setting.

World Index Number: NH/29-02-07
National Register of Historic Places: 09/22/1983

Whittier Covered Bridge (Bearcamp)
County: Carroll, New Hampshire
Township: Ossipee

GPS Position: N 43° 49.311' W071° 12.727'
Directions: From West Ossipee, head SW on NH-25 W of ME-25 for 0.5 mi and turn right onto Nudd Rd to find the bridge
Crosses: Bearcamp River
Carries: Covered Bridge Road

Builder: Jacob Berry
Year Built: C1870 (R1936) (R1983) (R2022)
Truss Type: Paddleford and Arch
Dimensions: 1 Span, 133 feet

Photo Tips: There are good views from all sides
Notes: As seen in the image above, the bridge was on blocks for 14 years. It was repaired and returned to it's original site in 2023

World Index Number: NH/29-02-08
National Register of Historic Places: 03/15/1984

Wentworth Country Club Covered Bridge
County: Carroll, New Hampshire
Township: Jackson

GPS Position: N 44°08.712' W 71°11.294'
Directions: From the town of Jackson, head SE on NH-16 S off main St and the bridge is 0.2 miles
Crosses: Ellis River
Carries: Cart path

Builder: Not known
Year Built: 1991
Truss Type: Warren
Dimensions: 1 Span, 115 feet

Photo Tips: Easy from all sides
Notes: Situated on the Wentworth Country Club, it is used by pedestrians and those with golf carts.

World Index Number: NH/29-02-13
National Register of Historic Places: Not Listed

Stoney Morrell Covered Bridge
County: Carroll, New Hampshire
Township: Conway

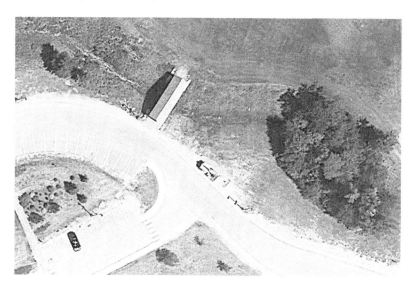

GPS Position: N 44° 00.392' W 071° 05.926'
Directions: From the town of Redstone, head west on US-302/Eastman Rd for 0.3 mi and turn left onto Eagle's Way/Mountain Valley Blvd/North-South Rd. Continue for 0.9 mi to see the bridge
Crosses: Ditch
Carries: Beside Eagle's Way road

Builder: Meg and Arnold Graton
Year Built: 1999 (M2015)
Truss Type: Town
Dimensions: 1 Span, 37 feet

Photo Tips: Very easy from all sides. The treed background would be beautiful in the fall
Notes: It was moved to Kennett High School in 2015

World Index Number: NH/29-02-14
National Register of Historic Places: Not listed

Ashuelot Covered Bridge (Upper Village)
County: Cheshire, New Hampshire
Township: Winchester

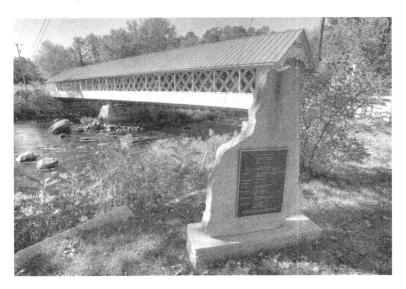

GPS Position: N 42° 46.644' W 72° 25.408'
Directions: From the town of Hinsdale, head northeast on NH-119 E/Canal St for 3.5 mi and turn right onto Gunn Mountain Rd to see the bridge
Crosses: Ashuelot River
Carries: Gunn Mountain Road

Builder: Nichols Montgomery Powers
Year Built: 1864 (R1999)
Truss Type: Town
Dimensions: 2 Span, 174 feet

Photo Tips: There are excellent setup points from all sides including some great 3/4 angle shots.
Notes: One of the finest covered bridges, it was built by one of the best builders, Nichols Montgomery Powers. It includes walkways on both sides.

World Index Number: NH/29-03-02
National Register of Historic Places: 2/20/1981

Coombs Covered Bridge
County: Cheshire, New Hampshire
Township: Winchester

GPS Position: N 42° 50.281' W 72° 21.649'
Directions: From the town of Winchester, head NW on NH-10 N/Keene Rd for 4.8 mi and turn left onto Coombs Bridge Rd and the bridge is 0.3 mi
Crosses: Ashuelot River
Carries: Coombs Bridge Rd.

Builder: Anthony Coombs
Year Built: 1837 (R1964) (R1971)
Truss Type: Town
Dimensions: 1 Span, 118 feet

Photo Tips: There is a very good river level side view which will include some colorful foliage in the right season.
Notes: One of the state's older bridges, it is unpainted and the weathered front and sides look great.

World Index Number: NH/29-03-03
National Register of Historic Places: 11/21/1976

West Swanzey Covered Bridge (Thompson)
County: Cheshire, New Hampshire
Township: Swanzey

GPS Position: N 42° 52.303' W 72° 19.688'
Directions: From the town of West Swanzey, head SW on California St from NH-10 for 0.2 mi and continue onto Main St and the bridge is a short distance
Crosses: Ashuelot River
Carries: Main St

Builder: Zadoc Taft
Year Built: 1832 (R1998)
Truss Type: Town
Dimensions: 2 Span, 151 feet

Photo Tips: The detail on the portals make these shots interesting.
Notes: The bridge was closed in 1990 but reopened after the 1998 repairs. It is characterized by a wide overhanging roof on the sides and includes a pedestrian walkway.

World Index Number: NH/29-03-04
National Register of Historic Places: 2/29/1980

Sawyer's Crossing Covered Bridge (Cresson)
County: Cheshire, New Hampshire
Township: Swanzey

GPS Position: N 42° 53.176' W 72° 17.173'
Directions: From the town of West Swanzey, head east on Sawyers Crossing Rd for 2.1 mi to find the bridge
Crosses: Ashuelot River
Carries: Sawyer's Crossing Road

Builder: Unknown
Year Built: 1859 (R1983) (R1996)
Truss Type: Town
Dimensions: 2 Span, 158 feet

Photo Tips: Side views are not easy but can be found with care.
Notes: Nicely detailed, it is looking in great condition after the most recent repairs. There are side timbers acting as buttresses, probably to keep the bridge from twisting in wind conditions, something Town truss bridges are prone to.

World Index Number: NH/29-03-05
National Register of Historic Places: 11/14/1978

Slate Covered Bridge
County: Cheshire, New Hampshire
Township: Swanzey

GPS Position: 42°50'50.6"N 72°20'25.3"W
Directions: From West Swanzey, head south on NH-10 S/W Swanzey Rd for 0.9 mi and turn left onto Westport Village Rd and the site is 0.4 mi
Crosses: Ashuelot River
Carries: Westport Village Road

Builder: Wright Construction
Year Built: 2001
Truss Type: Town
Dimensions: 1 Span, 142 feet

Photo Tips: Side views are not easy but can be found with care.
Notes: The original bridge from the 1800s was destroyed by fire in 1993. The current bridge opened in 2001 at a cost of almost $1,000,000

World Index Number: NH/29-03-06#2
National Register of Historic Places: Not listed

Carlton Covered Bridge (Whitcomb)
County: Cheshire, New Hampshire
Township: Swanzey

GPS Position: N 42° 51.277' W 72° 16.453'
Directions: From West Swanzey, head south on NH-10 S/W Swanzey Rd for 0.9 mi and turn left onto Westport Village Rd and the site is 0.4 mi
Crosses: South Branch of the Ashuelot River
Carries: Carlton Rd

Builder: Unknown
Year Built: 1869 (R1996)
Truss Type: Queen
Dimensions: 1 Span, 67 feet

Photo Tips: Easy from all sides with especially good side views.
Notes: After recent repairs, the bridge looks excellent. It has a barn red exterior with some white detailing on the portals.

World Index Number: NH/29-03-07
National Register of Historic Places: 6/10/1975

Happy Corner Covered Bridge
County: Coős, New Hampshire
Township: Pittsburg

GPS Position: N 45° 05.043' W 71° 18.814'
Directions: From the village of Happy Corner, head southwest on Hill Rd for 0.1 mi where you will find the bridge
Crosses: Perry Stream
Carries: Hill-Danforth Road

Builder: Unknown
Year Built: 1869
Truss Type: Paddleford and Arch
Dimensions: 1 Span, 78 feet

Photo Tips: Side views are difficult due to foliage obstructions but you can get to water level with care. The bridge currently has strings of light on them which may look good in the dark but aren't helpful in the daytime.
Notes: The wood is unpainted and textured with wear and the sides are uncovered from about four feet.

World Index Number: NH/29-04-01
National Register of Historic Places: Not listed

River Road Covered Bridge
County: Coős, New Hampshire
Township: Pittsburg

GPS Position: N 45° 04.355' W 71° 18.340'
Directions: From the village of happy Corner, head east on US-3 N for 0.7 mi and turn right onto River Rd where the bridge is 1.2 mi
Crosses: Perry Stream
Carries: River Road (Bypassed)

Builder: Captain Charles Richardson or his son
Year Built: 1858 (R1954) (R1983)
Truss Type: Queen
Dimensions: 1 Span, 51 feet

Photo Tips: Found in a natural setting with good setups from all sides including a side view from water level.
Notes: An unpainted and well weathered structure open for half the height of the sides, it has extended portals, and seems to have had a number of recent minor repairs.

World Index Number: NH/29-04-02
National Register of Historic Places: Not Listed

Clarksville Covered Bridge (Pittsburg)
County: Coös, New Hampshire
Township: Clarksville-Pittsburg

GPS Position: N 45° 03.280' W 71° 24.410'
Directions: From Pittsburg, head west on US-3 S/Main St for 0.8 mi and turn left onto Bacon Rd to see the bridge
Crosses: Connecticut River
Carries: Bacon Road
Builder: Unknown
Year Built: 1876
Truss Type: Paddleford and Arch
Dimensions: 1 Span, 89 feet

Photo Tips: There are excellent views all around and a particularly nice 3/4 view which takes advantage of the line of the guardrail and the background foliage.
Notes: This bridge lies on the line between Clarksville and Pittsburg townships and apparently this has caused some friction regarding paying the upkeep on this structure.

World Index Number: NH/29-04-03
National Register of Historic Places: Not listed

Groveton Covered Bridge
County: Coős, New Hampshire
Township: Northumberland

GPS Position: 44°35'44.2"N 71°30'37.6"W
Directions: From Northumberland, head south on Main St for 0.2 mi and turn left on bypassed section of US-3 and you will find the bridge
Crosses: Upper Ammonoosuc River
Carries: Bypassed section of US-3

Builder: Captain Charles Richardson or his son
Year Built: 1862 (R ca.1890) (R1954) (R1983)
Truss Type: Paddleford
Dimensions: 1+ Span, 138 feet (Pier added)

Photo Tips: Easy from all sides. Have a close look at the detail on the portals.
Notes: Surrounded by historic buildings, including an 1869 school and an 1853 church, it is an interesting spot to spend some time.

World Index Number: NH/29-04-05
National Register of Historic Places: Not listed

Stark Covered Bridge
County: Coős, New Hampshire
Township: Stark

GPS Position: N 44° 36.043' W 71° 24.464'
Directions: From of Stark, head SW on Northside Rd for 0.8 mi and turn right to stay on Northside Rd where you will see the bridge
Crosses: Upper Ammonoosuc River
Carries: Northside Road
Builder: Captain Charles Richardson or his son
Year Built: 1862 (R ca.1890) (R1954) (R1983)
Truss Type: Paddleford
Dimensions: 1+ Span, 138 feet (Pier added)

Photo Tips: Easy from all sides. Have a close look at the detail on the portals, similar to Groveton from the same builder
Notes: In the 1890s, the bridge was washed downstream and was brought back by oxen

World Index Number: NH/29-04-05
National Register of Historic Places: 12/8/1983

Mechanic Street Covered Bridge
County: Coős, New Hampshire
Township: Lancaster

GPS Position: 44°29'11.6"N 71°33'52.1"W
Directions: 71 Mechanic St, Lancaster
Crosses: Israel River
Carries: Mechanic Street

Builder: Unknown
Year Built: 1862 (R1867) (R2007)
Truss Type: Paddleford
Dimensions: 1 Span, 94 feet

Photo Tips: Excellent views from all around including an excellent side view.
Notes: An interesting aspect of this bridge are the graceful sweeping lines of the portals which extend over the sides. The sides are open for half the height.

World Index Number: NH/29-04-06
National Register of Historic Places: Not listed

Snyder Brook Covered Bridge
County: Coős County, New Hampshire
Township: Randolph

GPS Position: N 44° 22.276' W071° 17.116'
Directions: From the town of Gorham, head west on US-2 W/Lancaster Rd for 5.2 mi and you will see the bridge
Crosses: Snyder Brook
Carries: Abandoned Railway bed

Builder: Boston and Maine Railroad
Year Built: 1918
Truss Type: Boxed Pony Howe
Dimensions: 1 Span, 41 feet

Photo Tip: The best shots would seem to be from in front as well as a side view on the downstream side.
Notes: This bridge is known as a Boxed Pony. It has covered sides but not a top. This type is included in the "World Guide to Covered Bridges" and so we include them.

World Index Number: NH/29-04-P2
National Register of Historic Places: Not listed

Columbia Covered Bridge
County: Coős: New Hampshire and Essex, Vermont
Township: Columbia, NH and Lemington, VT

GPS Position: N 44° 51.159' W 71° 33.050'
Directions: From the town of Columbia, head SW on US-3 S for 0.2 mi and turn right onto Columbia Bridge Rd where the bridge is 0.2 mi
Crosses: Connecticut River
Carries: Columbia Bridge Rd.

Builder: Charles Babbitt
Year Built: 1912 (R1981)
Truss Type: Howe
Dimensions: 1 span, 146 feet

Photo Tip: There are good views from all sides, especially the north side in New Hampshire
Notes: This is one of three covered bridges which span the Connecticut River between New Hampshire and Vermont. It replaced a covered bridge which was destroyed by fire in 1911

World Index Number: NH/29-04-07 (NH) and 45-05-02 (VT)
National Register of Historic Places::12-12-1976

Mount Orne Covered Bridge
County: Coős (NH) and Essex (VT)
Township: Lancaster (NH) and Lunenburg (VT)

GPS Position: N 44° 27.634' W 71° 39.206'
Directions: From the village of South Lancaster, head SW on NH-135 S for 0.4 mi and continue straight onto Mt Orne Rd and the bridge
Crosses: Connecticut River
Carries: Mount Orne Road (Closed)
Builder: Berlin Iron Bridge Co.
Year Built: 1911 (R1969) (R1983)
Truss Type: Howe
Dimensions: 2 spans, 266 feet

Photo Tip: There are good views from the north side bank on both sides of the river
Note: This bridge replaced an open toll bridge built in the late 1800s. It was closed in 1983. It is said to produce a moaning sound in the right wind from the iron rods of its Howe truss.

World Index Number: NH/29-04-03#2 (NH) and 45-05-03#2 (VT)
National Register of Historic Places: 12/12/1976

Swiftwater Covered Bridge
County: Grafton, New Hampshire
Township: Bath

GPS Position: 44°08'04.4"N 71°57'02.3"W
Directions: 7 Porter Rd, Bath
Crosses: Wild Ammonoosuc River
Carries: Porter Road

Builder: Unknown
Year Built: 1849 (R1947) (R1977) (R1989) (R1999)
Truss Type: Paddleford
Dimensions: 2 Span, 158 feet

Photo Tips: There are excellent side views from the rocks below but be careful. Good 3/4 view as well. The white trim on the portals is a nice detail.
Notes: The bridge is unpainted except for portal trim and looks nicely weather textured. The portals are shingled. Two previous bridges at this site were destroyed by floods.

World Index Number: NH/29-05-02
National Register of Historic Places: 11/21/1976

Bath Covered Bridge
County: Grafton, New Hampshire
Township: Bath

GPS Position: N 44° 10.007' W 71° 58.084'
Directions: In the town of Bath, head southwest on W Bath Rd from US-302 for 0.1 mi and turn right onto Railroad St where you will find the bridge
Crosses: Ammonoosuc River
Carries: Bath Road

Builder: Unknown
Year Built: 1832 (R1920) (R2007) (R2014)
Truss Type: Burr Arch
Dimensions: 4 Span, 375 feet

Photo Tip: Go to the end opposite the town and you will gain easy access to the river edge. You will need a wide lens and might consider panoramic images. The church spire at the other side makes an interesting addition to the image.

Notes: This is one of the finest covered bridges in North America. Its setting is enhanced by waterfalls below as well as a typical white New England Church with spire at one end. Although this bridge has been here a long time, four previous bridges at this spot have been lost, three to floods and one to fire.

World Index Number: NH/29-05-03
National Register of Historic Places: 9/1/1976

Bath-Haverhill Covered Bridge (Woodsville)
County: Grafton, New Hampshire
Township: Bath-Haverhill

GPS Position: N 44° 09.252' W 72° 02.165'
Directions: 60 Woodsville Rd, Bath
Crosses: Ammonoosuc River
Carries: NH-135/Monroe Road (Bypassed)

Builder: Moses Abbott and Leonard Walker
Year Built: 1829 (R1973) (R1980) (R2003)
Truss Type: Town and Arch
Dimensions: 2 Span, 256 feet

Photo Tips: Easy views especially an excellent interior. You can get good side views from the sidewalk of the new bridge beside it, you will need a wide lens.
Notes: This is the oldest covered bridge in New Hampshire. The bridge is in good shape and is in a beautiful setting. It is closed to vehicle traffic. Admission

World Index Number: NH/29-05-04
National Register of Historic Places: 4/18/1977

Flume Covered Bridge
County: Grafton, New Hampshire
Township: Lincoln

GPS Position: N 44° 05.956' W 71° 40.599'
Directions: From the parking lot at Flume Reservation at Franconia SP, take the Flume Path for 200 feet and the bridge
Crosses: Pemigewasset River
Carries: Pedestrian trail
Builder: Unknown
Year Built: 1871 (R1951)
Truss Type: Paddleford
Dimensions: 1 Span, 52 feet

Photo Tip: Don't take the shuttle as you will not stop at the bridge. There are views from all sides although somewhat obstructed.
Notes: This is a good family destination. There is a another pedestrian only covered bridge called the Sentinel Pine as well as the attraction of the Flume River gorge. Admission

World Index Number: NH/29-05-05
National Register of Historic Places: Not listed

Bump Covered Bridge
County: Grafton, New Hampshire
Township: Campton

GPS Position: N 43° 48.859' W 71° 37.315'
Directions: From the town of Campton, head east on Perch Pond Rd for 0.3 mi and turn right to stay on Perch Pond Rd and continue 0.8 mi to the bridge
Crosses: Beebe River
Carries: Perch Pond Road
Builder: Arnold Graton
Year Built: 1972
Truss Type: Queen
Dimensions: 1 Span, 68 feet

Photo Tip: The side views are obstructed although you may find something passable when the leaves are off.
Notes: The Bump Bridge was built by Milton Graton in 1972 after he examined the previous bridge on this spot and found it could not be rehabilitated due to the deteriorated nature of its timbers.

World Index Number: NH/29-05-08#2
National Register of Historic Places: Not listed

Blair Covered Bridge
County: Grafton, New Hampshire
Township: Campton

GPS Position: N 43° 48.616' W 71° 39.991'
Directions: From the town of Campton, head south on New Hampshire Rte 175 S for 1.4 mi and turn right onto Blair Rd where the site is 0.6 mi
Crosses: Pemigewasset River
Carries: Blair Road
Builder: Unknown
Year Built: 1869 (R1977)
Truss Type: Long and Burr Arch
Dimensions: 2 Span, 293 feet

Photo Tip: You can reach river level from the SE corner for a good side view.
Notes: This bridge was rehabilitated by Milton Graton and his son Arnold in 1977. The Long truss system had Burr Arches added. It is a beautiful structure with windows in each span giving it a nice balance.

World Index Number: NH/29-05-09
National Register of Historic Places: Not listed

Smith Millennium Covered Bridge
County: Grafton, New Hampshire
Township: Plymouth

GPS Position: N 43° 46.517' W 71° 44.359'
Directions: From the town of Plymouth, head west on NH-25 W for 2.0 mi and turn right onto Smith Bridge Rd and the bridge is 0.5 mi
Crosses: Baker River
Carries: Smith Bridge Road
Builder: Stan Graton and Hayden Hillsgrove
Year Built: 2001 (Original 1850)
Truss Type: Long and Burr Arch
Dimensions: 1 Span, 167 feet
Photo Tip: There is an excellent 3/4 view from the viewing stand on the NE corner, and it is easy get to the river from the north side for a nice side view.
Notes: The original bridge was destroyed by fire in 1993. The replacement is an impressive structure with a pedestrian walkway and two lanes for vehicles. It is built to carry interstate highway loads.

World Index Number: NH/29-05-10#2
National Register of Historic Places: Not listed

Edgell Covered Bridge
County: Grafton, New Hampshire
Township: Lyme

GPS Position: N 43° 52.055' W 72° 09.903'
Directions: From the village of Orford, head SW on NH-10 S for 1.6 mi and turn right onto River Rd and the bridge is 1.0 mi
Crosses: Clay Brook
Carries: River Road

Builder: Walter Piper
Year Built: 1885 (R1936) (R1971) (R1982)
Truss Type: Town
Dimensions: 1 Span, 150 feet

Photo Tip: The side views are made difficult by obstructions but there are excellent 3/4 views.
Notes: In 1936 it was washed off its abutments and cables were installed to anchor it and these are still present. In 1982 the roof collapsed from a heavy snow load and it was repaired the same year.

World Index Number: NH/25-05-11
National Register of Historic Places: Not listed

Clark Covered Bridge (Pinsley Railroad)
County: Grafton, New Hampshire
Township: Lincoln

GPS Position: 44°03'05.6"N 71°41'16.0"W
Directions: From North Woodstock, head north on US-3 N/Main St for 1.3 mi and turn right onto Caboose Dr where the parking lt is
Crosses: Pemigewasset River
Carries: Interior rail

Builder: Unknown
Year Built: 1904 (M1965)
Truss Type: Howe
Dimensions: 1 Span, 120 feet

Photo Tip: You cannot walk into or through the bridge but there is a great 3/4 view.
Notes: This railroad bridge was originally located in Vermont between Barre and Montpelier. The owners of the Clark's Trading Post attraction acquired it from its abandoned position, moved it and rebuilt it in its present position in 1965.

World Index Number: NH/25-05-14
National Register of Historic Places: Not listed

Jack O'Lantern Resort Covered Bridge
County: Grafton, New Hampshire
Township: Woodstock

GPS Position: N 43° 56.955' W 71° 40.619'
Directions: From the town of Woodstock, head south on US-3 S for 3.0 mi to find the bridge
Crosses: Pond
Carries: None

Builder: Milton Graton
Year Built: 1986
Truss Type: Town
Dimensions: 1 Span, 79 feet
Photo Tips: Although found on a private golf course, you can photograph it from the parking lot.
Notes: This bridge is a replica of the Woodstock Covered Bridge which was destroyed by fire in 1971. It was built to half the size of the original and was completed by Milton Graton and then brought by train to the site.

World Index Number: NH/29-05-14
National Register of Historic Places: Not listed

Packard Hill Covered Bridge
County: Grafton, New Hampshire
Township: Lebanon

GPS Position: N 43° 38.298' W 72° 13.298'
Directions: In the town of Lebanon, head SW on Hardy Hill Rd after 0.1 mi turn left onto Riverside Dr to find the bridge
Crosses: Mascoma River
Carries: Riverside Drive

Builder: Arnold Graton Associates
Year Built: 1991
Truss Type: Town
Dimensions: 1 Span, 76 feet

Photo Tips: The sides are obstructed but the portal view is excellent with the bridge book ended by the walkway and a line of trees.
Notes: A Bailey bridge was replaced by this bridge in 1991 which was constructed by traditional methods. The Bailey bridge had replaced a Covered Bridge built in 1878

World Index Number: NH/29-05-50#2
National Register of Historic Places: Not listed

Squam River Covered Bridge
County: Grafton, New Hampshire
Township: Ashland

GPS Position: N 43° 43.092' W 71° 37.114'
Directions: From Ashland, head NW on US-3 S/Riverside Dr for 1.8 mi turn right onto River St and the bridge
Crosses: Squam Lake
Carries: River Road

Builder: Milton Graton and Sons
Year Built: 1990
Truss Type: Town
Dimensions: 1 Span, 61 feet

Photo Tip: There is a good side view from the beach.
Notes: This bridge came into existence because the people of the town of Ashland wanted it instead of a concrete and steel bridge that was being planned by the state. It is a one lane bridge which has a decided camber designed in.

World Index Number: NH/29-05-112
National Register of Historic Places: Not listed

Greenfield-Hancock Covered Bridge
County: Hillsborough, New Hampshire
Township: Greenfield-Hancock

GPS Position: N 42° 57.389' W 71° 56.069'
Directions: From Greenfield. head west on NH-136 W for 0.5 mi and continue straight onto Forest Rd where the bridge is 2.6 mi
Crosses: Contookook River
Carries: Forest Road

Builder: Henry Pratt
Year Built: 1937 (R1981) (R2001)
Truss Type: Pratt
Dimensions: 1 Span, 87 feet

Photo Tips: There is a good side view that can be reached from the SW corner.
Notes: The township line between Greenfield and Hancock falls in the center of the bridge as a sign shows. This bridge is a replacement of an 1852 bridge destroyed in a flood in 1936.

World Index Number: NH/29-06-02#2
National Register of Historic Places: Not listed

Blood Brook CB (Livermore, Old Russell Hill Road)
County: Hillsborough, New Hampshire
Township: Wilton

GPS Position: N 42° 49.766' W 71° 46.705'
Directions: From Wilton, head west on NH-31 S/State Rte 101 W and continue to follow State Rte 101 W where the bridge is 2.8 mi
Crosses: Blood Brook
Carries: Abandoned road

Builder: Unknown
Year Built: 1930s
Truss Type: Town Boxed Pony
Dimensions: 1 Span, 52 feet

Photo Tip: Easy from all sides. Look for the information sign on the end of one side.
Notes: This is one of three Boxed Pony bridges in New Hampshire. They have covered sides and no top. Since they are listed in the "World Guide to Covered Bridges", we also list them.

World Index Number: NH/29-06-P01
National Register of Historic Places: Not listed

Cileyville Covered Bridge (Bog Covered Bridge)
County: Merrimack, New Hampshire
Township: Andover

GPS Position: N 43° 25.855' W 71° 52.081'
Directions: From the town of Andover, head on NH-11/US-4 W and continue to follow NH-11 where the bridge is seen in 2.2 mi
Crosses: Blackwater River
Carries: NH-11

Builder: Print Atwood, Al Emerson and Charles Wilson
Year Built: 1887 (R1962) (R1982) (R2003)
Truss Type: Town
Dimensions: 1 Span, 53 feet

Photo Tip: This is a beautiful bridge and the large flag on the side will provide excellent images.
Notes: Originally called the Bog Covered Bridge, it was rebuilt in 2003. The large U.S flag on the side sets it off beautifully. It was bypassed in 1959 and became pedestrian use only

World Index Number: NH/29-07-01
National Register of Historic Places: 3/16/1989

Keniston Covered Bridge
County: Merrimack, New Hampshire
Township: Andover

GPS Position: N 43° 26.089' W 71° 50.177'
Directions: From Andover, head west on US-4 W/Main St and after 0.5 mi turn left onto Bridge Rd where the bridge is s short distance
Crosses: Blackwater River
Carries: Bridge St.

Builder: Albert Hamilton
Year Built: 1882 (R1949) (R1972) (R1981) (R2003)
Truss Type: Town
Dimensions: 1 Span, 62 feet

Photo Tip: There are excellent views from all sides especially a 3/4 view showing the open town trusses.
Notes: This bridge is unusual in that it has almost no sideboards and the town trusses are well shown. It is named for a family who were early settlers nearby

World Index Number: NH/29-07-02
National Register of Historic Places: 3/16/1989

Bement Covered Bridge
County: Merrimack, New Hampshire
Township: Bradford

GPS Position: N 43° 15.872' W 71° 57.161'
Directions: From the town of Bradford, head south on New Hampshire Rte 103 E and the bridge is 0.4 mi
Crosses: West Branch of the Warner River
Carries: Center Road
Builder: Stephen H. Long
Year Built: 1854 (R1947) (R1969) (R1987) (R1990) (R1921)
Truss Type: Long
Dimensions: 1 Span, 61 feet

Photo Tip: Side views are obstructed but there is a good 3/4 view from the east side.
Notes: The builder, Stephen Long, used the Long truss system for this bridge which was a support system which he patented. The 1987 repairs were necessitated by a vehicle damaging it. The 1921 rehabilitation included some new timbers and replacement of the north abutment

World Index Number: NH/29-07-03
National Register of Historic Places: 11/21/1976

Waterloo Station Covered Bridge
County: Merrimack, New Hampshire
Township: Warner

GPS Position: N 43° 17.302' W 71° 51.353'
Directions: From Warner, head NW on W Main St and continue on New Hampshire Rte 103 W for 0.8 mi. At the traffic circle, continue straight to stay on New Hampshire Rte 103 W for 1.1 mi and turn left onto Newmarket Rd. The bridge is 0.2 mi
Crosses: Warner River
Carries: Newmarket Road
Builder: Dutton Woods
Year Built: 1857 (R1970) (R1987)
Truss Type: Town
Dimensions: 1 Span, 76 feet

Photo Tip: There is a good 3/4 view down near water level.
Notes: This bridge is unpainted and the weathered texture and natural setting look very good, especially set off by the red roof.

World Index Number: NH/29-07-04
National Register of Historic Places: 11/21/1976

Dalton Covered Bridge (Joppa Road Bridge)
County: Merrimack, New Hampshire
Township: Warner

GPS Position: N 43° 16.631' W 71° 48.671'
Directions: From Warner, head southeast on E Main St for 0.1 mi and turn right onto W Joppa Rd where the bridge is a short distance
Crosses: Warner River
Carries: Joppa Hill Road

Builder: Joshua Sanborn
Year Built: 1853 (R1871) (R1964) (R1990)
Truss Type: Long and Queen
Dimensions: 1 Span, 77 feet

Photo Tip: There is an easy and excellent side view of this weathered bridge.
Notes: This bridge has an interesting truss system, a combination of the Long truss with Queenpost, although it has been wrongly described as a Kingpost and Queenpost in some sources.

World Index Number: NH/29-07-05
National Register of Historic Places: 11/21/1976

Contoocook Railroad Covered Bridge
County: Merrimack, New Hampshire
Township: Hopkinton

GPS Position: N 43° 13.375' W 71° 42.833'
Directions: In Contoocook, the bridge is just north of the intersection of Main and Maple streets
Crosses: Contoocook River
Carries: Main St. (Bypassed Section)

Builder: David Hazelton for the Boston & Maine Railroad.
Year Built: 1889 (R2007)
Truss Type: Double Town
Dimensions: 2 Span, 157 feet

Photo Tip: Easy views from front and sides and you can also photograph the interior.
Notes: This is the oldest surviving railroad covered bridge. It has had an interesting career, having washed off its abutments in 1936 and 1938, and from 1962 till 1990 it was used as a merchant's warehouse.

World Index Number: NH/29-07-07#2
National Register of Historic Places: 3/16/2006

Rowell Covered Bridge
County: Merrimack, New Hampshire
Township: Hopkinton

GPS Position: N 43° 11.539' W 71° 44.902'
Directions: From Contoocook, head south on NH-127 S/Maple St for 3.5 mi you find the bridge
Crosses: Contoocook River
Carries: Clement Hill Road
Builder: Horace, Enoch and Warren Childs
Year Built: 1853 (R1930) (R1965) (R1982) (R1995)
Truss Type: Long and Burr Arch
Dimensions: 1 Span (Center pier added), 167 feet

Photo Tip: With care when water levels are not high, you can go onto the rocks on the downstream side for an excellent side view.
Notes : Have a look at the interesting truss system, Long trusses sandwiching a Burr Arch. This bridge has a history of instability. Vibrations of cattle moving through it shook it off its abutments. The sides are open in the top half and the roof has a large overhang.

World Index Number: NH/29-07-08
National Register of Historic Places: 11/21/1976

Sulphite Railroad Covered Bridge
County: Merrimack, New Hampshire
Township: Franklin

GPS Position: N 43° 26.708' W 71° 38.119'
Directions: In Franklin, take the Winnipesaukee River Trail
from the entrance on Central St for 0.4 mi and you will see the
bridge. **Don't venture onto the bridge as it is in very poor
shape and dangerous.**
Crosses: Winnipesaukee River
Carries: Winnipesaukee River Trail
Builder: Boston and Maine Railroad
Year Built: 1896
Truss Type: Pratt
Dimensions: 3 Spans, 180 feet
Photo Tip: There is a good view from the side as you
approach on the trail.
Notes: This has often been called the "upside down" bridge
because the rail tracks were on top of what would be
considered the roof of the bridge. The bridge was destroyed
in a fire in 1980

World Index Number: NH/29-07-09
National Register of Historic Places: 6/11/1975

New England College Covered Bridge
County: Merrimack, New Hampshire
Township: Henniker

GPS Position: N 43° 10.646' W 71° 49.338'
Directions: Located at New England College in Henniker at 98 Bridge St.
Crosses: Contoocook River
Carries: Interior Road

Builder: Milton and Arnold Graton
Year Built: 1972
Truss Type: Town
Dimensions: 1 Span, 137 feet

Photo Tip: Excellent images from front and an interesting look from the interior including one with the trusses framing a stone arch bridge upstream.
Notes: The Gratons built this bridge in a completely authentic manner including moving it using a system of pulleys and a team of oxen. .

World Index Number:: NH/07-12
National Register of Historic Places: June 18, 1973

Wason Pond Covered Bridge
County: Rockingham, New Hampshire
Township: Chester

GPS Position: N 42° 58.904' W071° 12.971'
Directions: From the town of Chester, head northeast on NH-102 E toward Murphy Dr for 2.8 mi to find the bridge
Crosses: Wason Brook
Carries: Pedestrian trail

Builder: Eagle Scout Project
Year Built: 2011
Truss Type: Pratt Variant
Dimensions: 1 Span, 29 feet

Photo Tips: There is an excellent side view from the road which picks up the small waterfall under the bridge.

Notes: The project was organized by the Timber Framer's Guild and involved many local volunteers

World Index Number: NH/29-08-12
National Register of Historic Places: Not listed

Rollins Farm CB (Clement Road Ext. CB)
County: Stratford, New Hampshire
Township: East Vincent-West Vincent

GPS Position: N 43° 13.38' W 70° 51.12'
Directions: In Rollingsford, head northwest on Rollins Rd for 1.1 mi and walk 0.2 miles east opposite Clement Rd.
Crosses: Boston and Maine Railroad
Carries: Old Path

Builder: Boston & Maine Railroad
Year Built: 1904
Truss Type: Boxed Pony Queen
Dimensions: 1 Span, 43 feet

Photo Tip: Good views from the front and the graffiti and wear may add to the image.
Notes: This boxed pony bridge was built to cross the Boston and Maine Railroad but lies in disrepair. It is included in the "World Guide to Covered bridges" and we have therefore included it. The structure is in very poor shape

World Index Number: NH/29-09-P1
National Register of Historic Places: Not listed

Blacksmith Shop Covered Bridge
County: Sullivan, New Hampshire
Township: Cornish

GPS Position: N 43° 27.770' W 72° 21.237'
Directions: From Claremont, head north on NH-120 N/Hanover St for 6.5 mi and turn left onto Town House Rd where you find the bridge
Crosses: Mill Brook
Carries: Town House Road
Builder. James Tasker
Year Built: 1881 (R1983)
Truss Type: Multiple Kingpost
Dimensions: 1 Span, 96 feet

Photo Tip: Easy from all sides including a brook level side view.
Notes: The bridge was repaired by Milton Graton in 1983 and it was re-opened for pedestrian traffic only. It is unpainted and the weathered texture looks excellent, especially in the snow.

World Index Number: NH/29-10-01
National Register of Historic Places: Not listed

Dingleton Covered Bridge
County: Sullivan, New Hampshire
Township: Cornish

GPS Position: N 43° 27.868' W 72° 22.151'
Directions: From Claremont, head north on NH-120
N/Hanover St for 6.4 mi and turn left onto Town House Rd.
After 3.8 mi turn left onto Root Hill Rd to see the bridge
Crosses: Mill Brook
Carries: Root Hill Rd.

Builder: James Tasker
Year Built: 1882 (R1983)
Truss Type: Multiple Kingpost
Dimensions: 1 Span, 78 feet

Photo Tip: Good from all sides and an exceptional side view
showing the bridge perched on tall abutments.
Notes: An unpainted bridge in a quiet river valley, the top half
of the sides is open revealing the trusses. The 1983 repairs
were done by Milton Graton.

World Index Number: NH/29-10-02
National Register of Historic Places: 11/8/1978

Pier Railroad Covered Bridge (Chandler Station)
County: Sullivan, New Hampshire
Township: Newport

GPS Position: N 43° 21.721' W 72° 14.520'
Directions: From Newport, head west on Elm St for 0.8 mi
and turn right onto NH-11 W/New Hampshire Rte 103 W. In
1.7 mi turn left onto Chandlers Mill Rd and the bridge is 1.1 mi
Crosses: Sugar River
Carries: Chandlers Mill Road
Builder: Boston and Maine Railroad
Year Built: 1896 (R1909)
Truss Type: Double Town
Dimensions: 2 Span, 228 feet
Photo Tip: Good locations from the front and if you go back to
the edge of the road, you can get an impressive side view.
Notes: This is an impressive bridge, very heavily built with a
large double town truss system so that it could bear the weight
of heavy trains. The rails have been removed and the interior
now has a plank floor.

World Index Number: NH/29-10-03#2
National Register of Historic Places: 6/10/1975

Wright Railroad Covered Bridge
County: Sullivan, New Hampshire
Township: Newport

GPS Position: N 43° 21.533' W 72° 15.517'
Directions: From Newport, head NW on Elm St for 0.7 mi and turn right onto NH-11 W/New Hampshire Rte 103 W. After 1.7 mi turn left onto Chandlers Mill Rd and the bridge is 2.1 mi
Crosses: Sugar River
Carries: Railway right-of-way

Builder: Boston and Maine Railroad
Year Built: 1895 (R1906)
Truss Type: Double Town with Burr Arch
Dimensions: 1 Span, 124 feet

Photo Tip: There are beautiful portal images available and consider also the massive truss structure in the interior.
Notes: The weight of the trains needed a substantial structure and this bridge has a massive burr arch sandwiched between two heavy Town trusses. The bridge looks to be in good shape.

World Index Number: NH/29-10-04#2
National Register of Historic Places: 6/10/1975

Corbin Covered Bridge
County: Sullivan, New Hampshire
Township: Newport

GPS Position: N 43° 23.456' W 72° 11.699'
Directions: From Newport, head northwest on N Main St for 1.6 mi and turn left onto Corbin Rd where the site is 0.7 mi
Crosses: Sugar River
Carries: Corbin Rd

Builder: Arnold Graton and Associates
Year Built: 1994 (Rebuild of 1845 bridge)
Truss Type: Town
Dimensions: 1 Span, 102 feet

Photo Tip: Easy from all sides but especially side views from river level.
Notes:The original covered bridge was destroyed by arson in 1993. An authentic rebuild was completed in 1994 by Arnold Graton. The bridge is without windows like most early bridges and in a quiet setting.

World Index Number: NH/29-10-05#2
National Register of Historic Places: Not listed

McDermott Covered Bridge
County: Sullivan, New Hampshire
Township: Langdon

GPS Position: N 43° 10.206' W 72° 20.744'
Directions: From Alstead, head NE on NH-123 S/NH-12A S for 0.5 mi and turn left onto NH-123A E. After 1.3 mi take a slight left onto Crane Brook Rd where the bridge is 0.1 mi
Crosses: Cold River
Carries: Crane Brook Road (Bypassed)

Builder: Albert S. Granger
Year Built: 1869 (R1961)
Truss Type: Town with Arch
Dimensions: 1 Span, 86 feet

Photo Tip: With careful placement near the highway's edge you can get a good 3/4 view
Notes: This unpainted structure is well weathered but seems in reasonable shape. It was bypassed in 1964.

World Index Number: NH/29-10-06
National Register of Historic Places: Not listed

Prentiss Covered Bridge (Drewsville CB)
County: Sullivan, New Hampshire
Township: Langdon

GPS Position: N 43° 09.236' W 72° 23.611'
Directions: From Langdon, head west on Village Rd for 0.5 mi and continue straight onto Lower Cemetery Rd. After 0.6 mi continue onto Cheshire Turnpike and the site is 0.1 mi
Crosses: Great Brook
Carries: Cheshire Turnpike (Bypassed)

Builder: Albert S. Granger
Year Built: 1869 (R2000)
Truss Type: Town
Dimensions: 1 Span, 35 feet

Photo Tip: There is a good side view from the highway beside it but be careful of traffic.
Notes: This is New Hampshire's smallest Covered Bridge. It was bypassed in 1954.

World Index Number: NH/29-10-07
National Register of Historic Places: 5/24/1973

Meriden Covered Bridge (Mill Covered Bridge)
County: Sullivan, New Hampshire
Township: Plainfield

GPS Position: N 43° 33.197' W 72° 15.922'
Directions: From the village of Plainfield, head northwest on Main St toward Ballfield Rd for 0.9 mi to find the bridge
Crosses: Blood's Brook
Carries: Colby Hill Road

Builder: James Tasker
Year Built: 1880 (R1954) (R1963) (R1977) (R1985)
Truss Type: Multiple Kingpost
Dimensions: 1+ Span, 80 feet

Photo Tip: Sides views can be difficult and obstructed, with 3/4 views perhaps the best.
Notes: This bridge has suffered through calamities, Hurricane Carol damaged it in 1954 and the roof collapsed in 1977. It is unpainted and open on half of the sides.

World Index Number: NH/29-10-08
National Register of Historic Places: 8/27/1980

Blow-Me-Down Covered Bridge (Bayliss CB)
County: Sullivan, New Hampshire
Township: Cornish

GPS Position: N 43° 31.026' W 72° 22.439'
Directions: From Plainfield, head southwest on NH-12A S for 1.3 mi and turn left onto Mill Rd. After 0.3 mi turn slightly left onto Lang Rd and the bridge
Crosses: Blow-Me-Down Brook
Carries: Lang Rd.

Builder: James Tasker
Year Built: 1877 (R1980) (R2002)
Truss Type: Multiple Kingpost
Dimensions: 1 Span, 86 feet

Photo Tip: There may be a good side view which would include the waterfall but my visit in winter conditions made that too dangerous. It is in a quiet natural setting.
Notes: The bridge was repaired by Milton and Arnold Graton in 1980. It is unpainted and has a natural rustic appearance.

World Index Number: NH/29-10-10
National Register of Historic Places: 3/2/2001

Windsor-Cornish Covered Bridge
County: Sullivan (NH) and Windsor (VT)
Township: Cornish (NH) and Windsor (VT)

GPS Position: N 43° 28.375' W 72° 22.996'
Directions: From Cornish, head west on Town House Rd for 0.9 mi and take a slight right onto NH-12A N where the bridge is 0.3 mi
Crosses: Connecticut River
Carries: Bridge Street (VT) and Cornish Toll Rd. (NH)
Builder: James Tasker & Bela J. Fletcher
Year Built: 1866 (R1887) (R1892)(R1887) (R1925) (R1887) (R1938) (R1955) (R1977) (R1989) (R2001)
Truss Type: Town
Dimensions: 2 Span, 449 Feet, 2 Lanes
Photo Tip: There are good views from front and sides but watch for traffic. The New Hampshire side is a bit better
Notes: This is one of the finest covered bridges in North America with a toe in Vermont and the bulk in New Hampshire. It is the longest two span bridge in the world.

World Index Number: NH/29-10-09#2 and VT/45-14-1
National Register of Historic Places: 11/21/1976

New Hampshire Tours

The following self-guided tours provide efficient and leisurely day trips to the area bridges.

Carroll County 7 Bridges - 2 hours driving

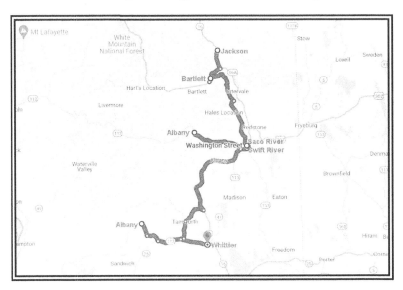

Jackson Covered Bridge	N 44° 08.499' W 71° 11.208'
Bartlett Covered Bridge	N 44° 05.707 W 71° 12.211'
Saco River Covered Bridge	N 43° 58.992' W 71° 07.019'
Swift River Covered Bridge	N 43° 59.066' W 71° 07.175'
Albany Covered Bridge	N 44° 00.342' W 71° 14.473'
Durgin Covered Bridge	N 43° 51.340' W 71° 21.866'
Whittier Covered Bridge	N 43° 49.311' W071° 12.72'

Cheshire County Tour - 6 Bridges, 40 minutes driving

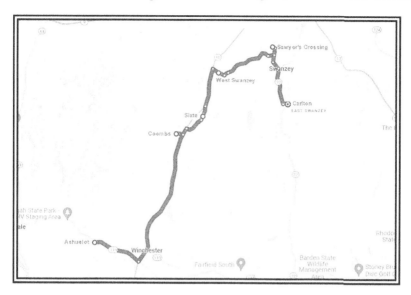

Ashuelot Covered Bridge	N 42° 46.644' W 72° 25.408'
Coombs Covered Bridge	N 42° 50.281' W 72° 21.649'
Slate Covered Bridge	N 42° 50.855' W 72° 20.411'
West Swanzey CB	N 42° 52.303' W 72° 19.688'
Sawyer's Crossing CB	N 42° 53.176' W 72° 17.173'
Carlton Covered Bridge	N 42° 51.277' W 72° 16.453'

Coős County Tour- 9 Bridges- 40 minutes driving

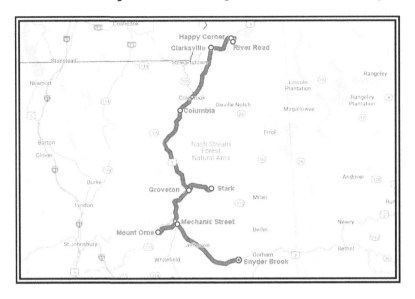

River Road Covered Bridge	N 45° 04.355' W 71° 18.340'
Happy Corner CB	N 45° 05.043' W 71° 18.814'
Clarksville Covered Bridge	N 45° 03.280' W 71° 24.410'
Columbia Covered Bridge	N 44° 51.159' W 71° 33.050'
Groveton Covered Bridge	N 44° 35.749' W 71° 30.684'
Stark Covered Bridge	N 44° 36.043' W 71° 24.464'
Mechanic Street CB	N 44° 29.194' W 71° 33.869'
Mount Orne CB	N 44° 27.634' W 71° 39.206'
Snyder Brook CB	N 44° 22.276' W 71° 17.11

Grafton County Tour 12 Bridges - 3 hour 30 min. Driving

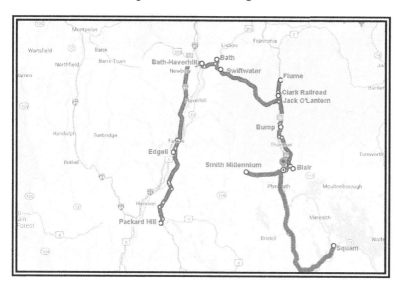

Packard Hill CB	N 43° 38.298' W 72° 13.298'
Edgell Covered Bridge	N 43° 52.055' W 72° 09.903'
Bath-Haverhill CB	N 44° 09.252' W 72° 02.165'
Bath Covered Bridge	N 44° 10.007' W 71° 58.084'
Swiftwater Covered Bridge	N 44° 08.074' W 71° 57.038'
Clark Railroad CB	N 44° 02.994' W 71° 41.273'
Flume Covered Bridge	N 44° 05.956' W 71° 40.599'
Jack O'Lantern CB	N 43° 56.955' W 71° 40.619'
Bump Covered Bridge	N 43° 48.859' W 71° 37.315'
Blair Covered Bridge	N 43° 48.616' W 71° 39.991'
Smith Millennium CB	N 43° 46.517' W 71° 44.359'
Squam River CB	N 43° 43.092' W 71° 37.114'

Merrimack County Tour 8 Bridges -1 hour 40 min
driving

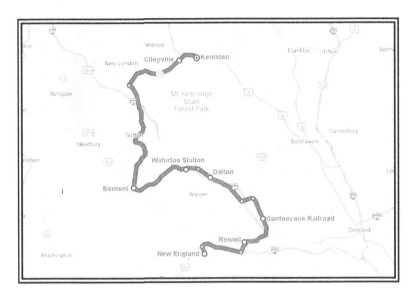

New England CB	N 43° 10.646' W 71° 49.338'
Rowell Covered Bridge	N 43° 11.539' W 71° 44.902'
Contoocook Railroad CB	N 43° 13.375' W 71° 42.833'
Dalton Covered Bridge	N 43° 16.631' W 71° 48.671'
Waterloo Station CB	N 43° 17.302' W 71° 51.353'
Bement Covered Bridge	N 43° 15.872' W 71° 57.161'
Cileyville Covered Bridge	N 43° 25.855' W 71° 52.081'
Keniston Covered Bridge	N 43° 26.089' W 71° 50.177'

Sullivan County Tour 9 Bridges – 2 hours 30 min driving

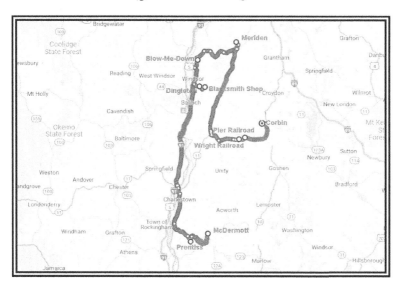

McDermott CB	N 43° 10.206' W 72° 20.744'
Prentiss Covered Bridge	N 43° 09.236' W 72° 23.611'
Dingleton Covered Bridge	N 43° 27.868' W 72° 22.151'
Blacksmith Shop CB	N 43° 27.770' W 72° 21.237'
Blow-Me-Down CB	N 43° 31.026' W 72° 22.439'
Meriden Covered Bridge	N 43° 33.197' W 72° 15.922'
Wright Railroad CB	N 43° 21.533' W 72° 15.517'
Pier Railroad CB	N 43° 21.721' W 72° 14.520'
Corbin Covered Bridge	N 43° 23.456' W 72° 11.699'

Vermont County Map

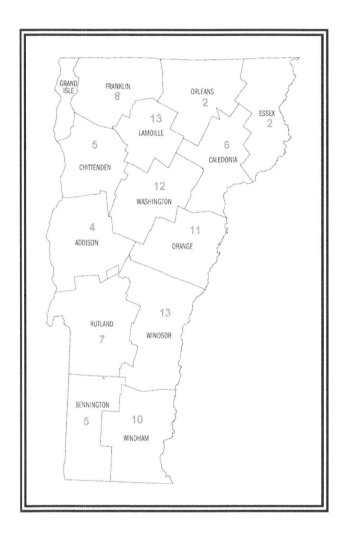

Spade Farm Covered Bridge (Old Hollow)
County: Addison, Vermont
Township: Ferrisburgh

GPS Position: N 44° 12.415' W 73° 14.885'
Directions: From the town of North Ferrisburg go west on Old Hollow Road and turn left on US-7 after 0.7 miles. The bridge is on the west side of the road after 1.3 miles
Crosses: Pond
Carries: Pedestrian walkway
Builder: Justin Miller
Year Built: 1850s (M1958) (R1999) (R2003)
Truss Type: Town
Dimensions: 1 Span, 85 Feet
Photo Tips: Easy from all sides. It has some interesting things inside it.
Notes: Originally located on Lewis Creek in North Ferrisburgh, Vermont, it was moved to its present location in 1958. While it is on private property, visitors are allowed. A sign on it indicates it was built in 1824, but research indicates it was more likely in the 1850s

World Index Number: VT/45-01-02
National Register of Historic Places: Not listed

Halpin Covered Bridge (High)
County: Addison, Vermont
Township: Middlebury-New Haven

GPS Position: N 44° 03.002' W 73° 08.459'
Directions: From of New Haven, go south on US-7/Ethan Allen Highway and, after 4.7 miles, turn left on River Rd. After a mile, turn right on Halpin Rd. and then left on Halpin Covered Bridge Road. The bridge site is about 0.3 miles
Crosses: New Haven River
Carries: Halpin Covered Bridge Road
Builder: Not known
Year Built: 1840 (R1994)
Truss Type: Town
Dimensions: 1 Span, 66 Feet
Photo Tips: Easy front and 3/4 view but a side view is a bit dodgy due to the height of the gorge
Notes: At 41 feet, this is Vermont's highest bridge over it's water course. It is also one of the oldest. It was built to allow access to a marble quarry and the original abutments were made of marble.

World Index Number: VT/45-01-03
National Register of Historic Places: September 10, 1974

Pulp Mill Covered Bridge (Paper Mill)
County: Addison, Vermont
Township: Middlebury-Weybridge

GPS Position: N 44° 01.453' W 73° 10.663'
Directions: From Middlebury take Elm St east off US-7 for 0.2 miles and turn right on Seymour St. After 0.6 miles continue left onto Pulp Mill Bridge Rd where you will find the bridge
Crosses: Otter Creek
Carries: Pulp Mill Bridge Road
Builder: Not known
Year Built: 1853-1854 (R1979) (R2002) (R2012)
Truss Type: Multiple King with Burr Arch
Dimensions: 1+ span, 199 Feet
Photo Tips: There is a side view near the dam side on the west side. Be careful
Notes: Sometimes called Vermont's oldest covered bridge with build date c1820 but the World Guide to Covered Bridges lists it as 1853-1854.It is one of a few two lane bridges in North America which still carries vehicle traffic and it also has a pedestrian walkway.

World Index Number: VT/45-01-04
National Register of Historic Places: September 10, 1974

East Shoreham Railroad CB (Rutland Railroad)
County: Addison, Vermont
Township: Shoreham

GPS Position: N 43° 51.561' W 73° 15.363'
Directions: From Shoreham go south on VT-22A for 0.5 mi and take the 1st left onto Richville Rd. After 3.2 miles turn right on Shoreham Depot Rd and a parking lot and bridge is 0.9 mi
Crosses: Lemon Fair River
Carries: Abandoned rail line
Builder: Rutland Railroad Company
Year Built: 1897 (R1983) (R2007)
Truss Type: Howe
Dimensions: 1 Span, 109 Feet

Photo Tips: The portal image as you approach gives a good idea of the size and will include some of the remaining tracks
Notes: One of two covered railroad bridges surviving in Vermont, this is a wonderful structure which ceased rail traffic in 1951. Due to the much heavier loads they carried, the railway bridges were more massively built

World Index Number: VT/45-01-05
National Register of Historic Places: June 13, 1974

Bridge At The Green CB (Arlington)
County: Bennington, Vermont
Township: Arlington

GPS Position: N 43° 06.272' W 73° 13.208'
Directions: From the town of West Arlington, the bridge is off VT-313/ Batten Kill Rd on Covered Bridge Rd
Crosses: Batten Kill
Carries: Covered Bridge Rd

Builder: Not known
Year Built: 1852 (R1974) (R1980) (R1982) (R2012)
Truss Type: Town
Dimensions:1 Span, 80 Feet

Photo Tips: Good views from all sides.
Notes: Found at the entrance to the Norman Rockwell homestead, it is a pleasant place for a family outing or picnic. In January 2012 there were repairs being made from the effects of Hurricane Irene as you can see in the image

World Index Number: VT/45-02-01
National Register of Historic Places: August 28, 1973

Henry Covered Bridge
County: Bennington, Vermont
Township: Bennington

GPS Position: N 42° 54.737' W 73° 15.288'
Directions: From the town of North Bennington, go south on Buckley Road, continuing on Water St., for about 1.3 miles. Turn left on River Road and the bridge is a short distance
Crosses: Walloomsac River
Carries: River Road

Builder: Blow and Cote
Year Built: 1989 (Original 1840)
Truss Type: Town
Dimensions: 1 Span, 121 Feet

Photo Tips: A nice quiet setting with easy views from all sides
Notes: None of the original materials was used in the rebuild. The original had its Town trusses doubled to increase its load capacity but the current bridge is a single Town truss

World Index Number: VT/45-02-02#2
National Register of Historic Places: Not listed

Paper Mill Covered Bridge (Bennington)
County: Bennington, Vermont
Township: Bennington

GPS Position: N 42° 54.776' W 73° 13.992'
Directions: In the town of North Bennington go south on Murphy Road off of VT-67A/ North Bennington Road and the bridge is a short distance
Crosses: Walloomsac River
Carries: Murphy Road
Builder: Blow and Cote (Original Charles F. Sears)
Year Built: 2000 (Original 1889)
Truss Type: Town
Dimensions: 1 Span, 126 Feet

Photo Tips: Watch for posted private property but there are good vantage points for the front and sides
Notes: The original bridge was demolished in 1999 and its replacement was completed in 2000 as the cost of repairs exceeded the price of a new bridge. It is built in an authentic manner and the fresh barn red paint job looks excellent

World Index Number: VT/45-02-03#2
National Register of Historic Places: Not listed

Silk Covered Bridge (Locust Grove)
County: Bennington, Vermont
Township: Bennington

GPS Position: N 42° 54.577' W 73° 13.519'
Directions: In North Bennington go south on Silk Rd off of VT-67A/ North Bennington Rd and the bridge is a short distance
Crosses: Walloomsac River
Carries: Silk Road

Builder: Benjamin Sears
Year Built: Ca1840 (R1952) (R1985) (R1991) (R1993)
Truss Type: Town
Dimensions: 1 Span, 88 Feet

Photo Tips: Easy from all sides.
Notes: This is a lovely bridge in a natural setting. The barn red paint is nicely set off by white on the portal trim

World Index Number: VT/45-02-04
National Register of Historic Places: August 28, 1973

Chiselville Covered Bridge
County: Bennington, Vermont
Township: Sunderland

GPS Position: N 43° 04.345' W 73° 07.959'
Directions: From the town of East Arlington Take Maple St. and continue on Sunderland Hill Rd northeast and the bridge site is about 1 mile
Crosses: Batten Kill
Carries: Sunderland Hill Rd

Builder: Daniel Oatman
Year Built: 1870 (R1972) (R1996)
Truss Type: Town
Dimensions: 2 Span, 117 Feet, steel pier was added in 1973

Photo Tips: Front and 3/4 shots only. The river is 40 feet below down steep banks making side views difficult.
Notes: Named after a Chisel Factory which was formerly in the area. It replaced a bridge washed out in 1869

World Index Number: VT/45-02-05
National Register of Historic Places: Not listed

Greenbanks Hollow Covered Bridge
County: Caledonia, Vermont
Township: Danville

Township: West St. Clair
County: Bedford
GPS Position: N 44° 22.644' W 72° 07.328'
Directions: From Danville take Brainerd St. south from US-2 and continue on Greenbanks Hollow Road. You will find the bridge after 2.7 miles.
Crosses: Joe's Brook
Carries: Greenbanks Hollow Road
Builder: Not known
Year Built: 2002 (Original 1886)
Truss Type: Queenpost
Dimensions: 1 Span, 74 Feet

Photo Tips: Open from all sides
Notes: The 2002 rebuild made many changes to take out non-authentic elements. It is in a quiet spot and looks great with its partially open sides

World Index Number: VT/45-03-01#2
National Register of Historic Places: Not listed

Schoolhouse Covered Bridge
County: Caledonia, Vermont
Township: Lyndon

GPS Position: N 44° 30.977' W 72° 00.591'
Directions: From the town of Lyndon go south on US-5 past I-91 and after 0.8 miles turn right on South Wheelock Rd. The parking lot for the bridge is a short distance
Crosses: South Wheelock Branch of Passumpsic River
Carries: South Wheelock Rd. (Bypassed)

Builder: J.C. Jones, Lee Goodell and John Clement
Year Built: 1879 (R1959) (R1971)
Truss Type: Queenpost
Dimensions: 1 Span, 42 Feet

Photo Tips: Easy from all sides.
Notes: The trusses have been enclosed and painted while there is only one walkway instead of the original two. A very nice looking bridge in a park like setting

World Index Number: VT/45-03-03
National Register of Historic Places: March 31, 1971

Chamberlin Mill Covered Bridge (Whitcomb)
County: Caledonia, Vermont
Township: Lyndon

GPS Position: N 44° 31.008' W 72° 01.006'
Directions: From I-91 take Exit 23, south of the town of Lyndon and go east on US-5 for 0.4 miles and then turn right onto Chamberlin Bridge Rd. The bridge is a short distance
Crosses: Passumpsic River
Carries: Chamberlin Bridge Rd.
Builder: Not known
Year Built: 1881 (R2002)
Truss Type: Queen
Dimensions: 1 Span, 66 Feet

Photo Tips: Easy portal views although you need to watch for traffic. There are no easy side views.
Notes: The original bridge was an open one which was covered in 1881. At one point it seems to have been relegated to a walkway and wood storage but it currently carries vehicle traffic.

World Index Number: VT45-03-04
National Register of Historic Places: July 30, 1974

Sanborn Covered Bridge (Centre)
County: Caledonia, Vermont
Township: Lyndon

GPS Position: N 44° 32.628' W 72° 00.055'
Directions: From Lyndon go to the north end on US-5. The bridge site is just south of the intersection with Stevens Loop
Crosses: Passumpsic River
Carries: Private lane

Builder: Not known
Year Built: 1867 (M1960) (R2002) (R2013)
Truss Type: Paddleford
Dimensions: 1 Span, 117 Feet

Photo Tips: Easy from all sides
Notes: One of only three Vermont bridges using the Paddleford Truss. Privately owned, it was moved to this location in 1960.

World Index Number: VT/45-03-05
National Register of Historic Places: June 20, 1974

Miller's Run Covered Bridge (Bradley)
County: Caledonia, Vermont
Township: Lyndon

GPS Position: N 44° 32.533' W 72° 00.596'
Directions: From the village of Lyndon Center go north on Center St. for 0.2 miles where you will see the site
Crosses: Miller's Run
Carries: Center St.

Builder: Not known (E.H. Stone Original Plans)
Year Built: 1995 (Original 1878)
Truss Type: Queenpost
Dimensions: 1 Span, 56 Feet

Photo Tips: Good views from all sides but watch for traffic
Notes: This bridge was restored using some of the timbers from the original 1878 bridge. It has a walkway for pedestrians and continues to serve vehicle traffic..

World Index Number: VT/45-03-06#2
National Register of Historic Places: Not listed

Old Burrington Covered Bridge (Randall)
County: Caledonia, Vermont
Township: Lyndon

GPS Position: N 44° 33.198' W 71° 58.165'
Directions: From Lyndon take US-5/Main St. north and continue on VT-114/ Burke Rd for 1.7 miles and turn right onto Burrington Bridge Road.The bridge is a short distance.
Crosses: East Branch of the Passumpsic River
Carries: Burrington Bridge Road

Builder: Not known
Year Built: 1865
Truss Type: Queen
Dimensions: 1 Span, 68 Feet

Photo Tips: Easy from all sides
Notes: The bridge has been bypassed and in 2011 was not in the best condition

World Index Number: VT/45-03-07
National Register of Historic Places: June 13, 1974

Holmes Covered Bridge (Lake Shore)
County: Chittenden, Vermont
Township: Charlotte

GPS Position: N 44° 19.970' W 73° 16.940'
Directions: From of Charlotte, take Ferry Rd west and, after 0.6 mi, turn right on Lake Rd. The bridge site is then 1.8 miles
Crosses: Holmes Creek
Carries: Lake Road

Builder: Leonard Sherman
Year Built: 1870 (R1993)
Truss Type: King with Tied Arch
Dimensions: 1 Span, 41 Feet

Photo Tips: Easy views from all sides.
Notes: Found on the shore of Lake Champlain, it provides a beautiful setting. There is a municipal swimming area nearby, ideal for a family outing and picnic

World Index Number: VT/45-04-01
National Register of Historic Places: September 6, 1974

Seguin Covered Bridge (Upper, Brown's)
County: Chittenden, Vermont
Township: Charlotte

GPS Position: N 44° 17.333' W 73° 09.002'
Directions: From Monkton Ridge go north on Monkton Rd and take a slight right onto Silver St. After 0.4 miles turn left on Rotax Rd and continue for 1.9 miles where you turn right on Roscoe Rd. The bridge site is about 1.8 miles
Crosses: Lewis Creek
Carries: Roscoe Road

Builder: Not known
Year Built: 1850 (R1949) (R1978) (R1994) (R2002) (2016)
Truss Type: Multiple King with Burr Arch
Dimensions: 1 Span, 71 Feet

Photo Tips: All sides are available
Notes: Very similar in construction to nearby Quinlin Covered Bridge and may well have had the same builder. In a nice quiet setting

World Index Number: VT/45-04-02
National Register of Historic Places: September 6, 1974

Quinlin Covered Bridge (Lower)
County: Chittenden, Vermont
Township: Charlotte

GPS Position: N 44° 16.559' W 73° 11.047'
Directions: From Charlotte go east on Ferry Rd and turn right on US-7/ Ethan Allen Highway. After 2.5 miles turn left onto State Park Rd and after a further 0.6 miles turn right onto Mt Philo Rd. After 0.9 miles make a sharp right on Spear St and continue 2.1 miles to the bridge site
Crosses: Lewis Creek
Carries: Spear St

Builder: Not known
Year Built: 1849 (R1950) (R1994) (R2013)
Truss Type: Multiple King with Burr Arch
Dimensions: 1 Span 86 Feet

Photo Tips: Easy from all sides..
Notes: On a quiet road although the creek can flood at times. Steel beams were installed under the floor at some point

World Index Number: VT/45-04-03
National Register of Historic Places: September 10, 1974

Westford Covered Bridge (Brown's River)
County: Chittenden, Vermont
Township: Charlotte

GPS Position: N 44° 36.748' W 73° 00.462'
Directions: In the town of Westford go east off VT-128 on Cambridge Road. The bridge site is a short distance
Crosses: Brown's River
Carries: Cambridge Road

Builder: Not known
Year Built: 1837 (R1976) (R1987) (R2001)
Truss Type: Multiple King with Burr Arch
Dimensions: 1 Span, 97 Feet

Photo Tips: Good 3/4 views available
Notes: The bridge was closed to traffic in 1965 and it was feared it would collapse. Through the years attempts to raise funds and save it were made and it was finally return to a bypassed section in 2001 after being rebuilt

World Index Number: VT/45-04-05
National Register of Historic Places: Not listed

Cambridge Village CB (Museum)
County: Chittenden, Vermont
Township: Shelburne

GPS Position: N 44° 22.397' W 73° 13.859'
Directions: In the town of Shelburne, the bridge is located at the Shelburne Museum just off US-7/ Shelburne Rd between Harbor Rd and Bostwick Rd.
Crosses: Burr Pond
Carries: Cambridge Road (Bypassed)
Builder: Farewell Wetherly
Year Built: 1845 (M1951) (R1998)
Truss Type: Multiple King with Burr Arch
Dimensions: 1 Span, 163 Feet

Photo Tips: There is an admission charge although you can take pictures from the public street
Notes: Originally located in Cambridge, Vermont, it was bypassed by a steel bridge, and was donated to the Shelburne Museum. It was dismantled and moved to its present location in 1951.

World Index Number: VT/45-04-06
National Register of Historic Places: Not listed

Columbia Covered Bridge
County: Coos County, NH and Essex, VT
Township: Columbia, NH and Lemington, VT

GPS Position: N 44° 51.159' W 71° 33.050'
Directions: Take Vermont-102 south from the Lemington area and turn left on Bridge St. The bridge is a short distance. From the New Hampshire side, take New Hampshire-26/ Us-3 south from Columbia and turn right on the Columbia Bridge Rd. and follow a short way to the end
Crosses: Connecticut River
Carries: Columbia Bridge Rd.
Builder: Charles Babbitt
Year Built: 1912 (R1981)
Truss Type: Howe
Dimensions: 1 span, 146 feet

Photo Tips: There are good views from all sides, especially the north side in New Hampshire.
Notes: This is one of three covered bridges which span the Connecticut River between New Hampshire and Vermont.

World Index Number: VT/45-05-02 and NH/29-04-07
National Register of Historic Places: December 12, 1976

Mount Orne Covered Bridge
County: Coos County, NH and Essex, VT
Township: Columbia, NH and Lemington, VT

GPS Position: N 44° 27.634' W 71° 39.206'
Directions: From Lunenburg, VT take US-2 east and turn right on River Rd. After 0.3 mi, you will see the bridge entrance on the left. From Lancaster, NH go south on NH-135/ Elm St. and you will reach the bridge entrance in a bit more than 5 miles.
Crosses: Connecticut River
Carries: Mount Orne Road
Builder: Berlin Iron Bridge Co.
Year Built: 1911 (R1938) (R1969) (R1983)
Truss Type: Howe
Dimensions: 2 spans, 266 feet
Photo Tips: There are good views from the north side bank on both sides of the river
Notes: This bridge replaced an open toll bridge built in the late 1800s. It was closed in 1983. The bridge was re-opened in 2012

World Index Number: VT/45-05-03#2 and NH/29-04-03#2
National Register of Historic Places: December 12, 1976

Hopkins Covered Bridge
County: Franklin, Vermont
Township: Enosburg

GPS Position: N 44° 55.229' W 72° 40.366'
Directions: From the town of East Berkshire take State Route 118/ Montgomery Rd. east for 2.2 miles and then take a right onto Hopkins Bridge Road where you will see the bridge
Crosses: Trout River
Carries: Hopkins Bridge Road

Builder: Sheldon & Savannard Jewett
Year Built: 1999 (Original 1875)
Truss Type: Town
Dimensions: 1 Span, 90 Feet

Photo Tips: Easy views from all sides
Notes: A rebuild of the structure was made in 1999 and the bridge looks in excellent condition

World Index Number: VT/45-06-01#2
National Register of Historic Places: Not listed

Maple Street CB (Village, Lower)
County: Franklin, Vermont
Township: Fairfax

GPS Position: N 44° 39.803' W 73° 00.630'
Directions: In the town of Fairfax take Maple St south off VT-104/ Main St. and the bridge is about 0.2 miles
Crosses: Mill Brook
Carries: Maple St

Builder: Kingsbury and Stone
Year Built: 1865 (R1975) (R1991) (R1998) (R2002)
Truss Type: Town
Dimensions: 1 Span, 57 Feet

Photo Tips: Although right in the town of Fairfax, it is in a natural setting, easy views from front and sides
Notes: The 1927 flood which destroyed many covered bridges, washed this one downstream and when it was returned it was said to have been restored with the west end facing east, and has caused a slight permanent lean

World Index Number: VT/45-06-02
National Register of Historic Places: November 5, 1974

East Fairfield Covered Bridge
County: Franklin, Vermont
Township: Fairfield

GPS Position: N 44° 47.168' W 72° 51.719'
Directions: In the town of East Fairfield, look for Bridge St. just off VT-36. The bridge site is only a short distance
Crosses: Black Creek
Carries: Bridge St.

Builder: Not known
Year Built: 1865 (R1940s) (R1967) (R1974) (R2009)
Truss Type: Queen
Dimensions: 1 Span, 67 Feet

Photo Tips: There are good views from all sides. Black Creek provides good reflections in side views
Notes: Notes: Since the completion of the 2009 repairs, this bridge is again open for vehicle traffic and looks in excellent condition

World Index Number: VT/45-06-03
National Register of Historic Places: November 19, 1974

Comstock Covered Bridge
County: Franklin, Vermont
Township: Montgomery

GPS Position: N 44° 53.969' W 72° 38.669'
Directions: From the town of Montgomery, go west on State Route 118 for 2.3 miles and turn left onto Comstock Bridge Rd. The bridge site is a short distance
Crosses: Trout River
Carries: Comstock Bridge Rd

Builder: Sheldon and Savannard Jewett
Year Built: 1883 (R1998) (R2004)
Truss Type: Town
Dimensions: 1 Span, 69 feet
Photo Tips: There are easy views all around but look for a longer shot from the side with the river in the foreground
Notes: This is a very nice looking structure with unpainted sides and white portals and interior weather panels

World Index Number: VT/45-06-04
National Register of Historic Places: November 19, 1974

Fuller Covered Bridge (Post Office)
County: Franklin, Vermont
Township: Montgomery

GPS Position: N 44° 54.199' W 72° 38.376'
Directions: From Montgomery, take Main St./ State Route 118 northwest for 2.3 mi and turn right onto South Richford Rd. The bridge is about 0.2 mi, near the intersection of Brook Rd
Crosses: Black Falls Brook
Carries: South Richford Road
Builder: Blow& Cote (Original Sheldon and Savanard Jewett)
Year Built: 2002 (Original 1890) (R2002)
Truss Type: Town
Dimensions: 1 Span, 50 Feet

Photo Tips: There are easy views from the fronts and sides
Notes: This is a bridge which has seen a few disasters from floods, truck damage, and even a Powder Post Beatle infestation. It seems to be a survivor and it has had a recent extensive renovation which included the removal of a non-authentic steel I-beam

World Index Number: VT/45-06-05#2
National Register of Historic Places:Not listed

Hutchins Covered Bridge
County: Franklin, Vermont
Township: Montgomery

GPS Position: N 44° 51.520' W 72° 36.769'
Directions: From of Montgomery, go south on State Route 118/ Main St. for 1.2 miles and then turn right onto Hutchins Bridge Rd. The bridge site is a short distance.
Crosses: South Branch Trout River
Carrles: Hutchins Bridge Rd

Builder: Sheldon and Savanard Jewett
Year Built: 1883 (R1969) (R2002)
Truss Type: Town
Dimensions: 1 Span, 77 Feet

Photo Tips: This bridge is in a beautiful natural setting. There are large steel beams that make some images a problem
Notes: Sheldon and Savanard Jewett built all of the bridges that survive in the Montgomery area. This bridge has closed awaiting repair

World Index Number: VT/45-06-07
National Register of Historic Places: December 30,1974

Longley Covered Bridge (Harnois, Head)
County: Franklin, Vermont
Township: Montgomery

GPS Position: N 44° 54.438' W 72° 39.333'
Directions: From the town of East Berkshire, take State Route 118/ Montgomery Rd southeast for 3.6 miles and turn right onto Longley Bridge Rd. The bridge is a short distance
Crosses: Trout River
Carries: Longley Bridge Rd

Builder: Sheldon and Savanard Jewett
Year Built: 2017 (Original 1863) (R1979) (R1992)
Truss Type: Town
Dimensions: 1 Span, 85 Feet

Photo Tips: Easy views from all sides
Notes: Found in a quiet country setting, the white portals look great against the weathered unpainted sides.

World Index Number: VT/45-06-08#2
National Register of Historic Places: Not listed

West Hill Covered Bridge (Creamery)
County: Franklin, Vermont
Township: Montgomery

GPS Position: N 44° 52.069' W 72° 38.868'
Directions: From Montgomery go west on Main St/ State Route 118 for 2.6 mi and turn left onto Hill West Rd. After 2.4 miles turn right on Creamery Bridge Rd and the bridge is a short distance. If the roads are icy, you might be safer to park at the top and walk down
Crosses: West Hill Brook
Carries: Creamery Bridge Road
Builder: Sheldon and Savanard Jewett
Year Built: 1883 (R2000) (R2009)
Truss Type: Town
Dimensions: 1 Span, 59 Feet

Photo Tips: There are side views with care and easy portal views
Notes: This bridge had been closed to traffic in 1994 but the 2009 renovation has allowed it to re-open

World Index Number: VT/45-06-09
National Register of Historic Places: December 31, 1974

Grist Mill CB (Scott, Bryan, Canyon)
County: Lamoille, Vermont
Township: Cambridge

GPS Position: N 44° 38.195' W 72° 49.531'
Directions: From Jeffersonville, take Mill St./ Vt-108 south for 0.7 mi and then left on Canyon Rd. The site is about 0.5 miles
Crosses: Canyon Rd.
Carries: Brewster River

Builder: Not known
Year Built: 1872 (R1952) (R1970) (R2004)
Truss Type: Multiple Kingpost with Burr Arch
Dimensions: 1 Span, 85 feet

Photo Tips: There is an excellent side view from river level
Notes: One of the bridges names is for a grist mill that used to be located nearby

World Index Number: VT/45-08-01
National Register of Historic Places: June 13, 1974

Cambridge Junction CB (Poland, Station)
County: Lamoille, Vermont
Township: Cambridge

GPS Position: N 44° 39.088' W 72° 48.798'
Directions: from the Town of Jeffersonville, take VT-108 north 0.4 miles and turn right on VT-109, and after 0.8 miles, another right onto Cambridge Junction Rd. to the bridge
Crosses: Lamoille River
Carries: Cambridge Junction Rd.(Closed)

Builder: George W. Holmes
Year Built: 1887 (R2004)
Truss Type: Multiple Kingposts with Burr Arch
Dimensions: 1 Span, 153 feet

Photo Tips: There are probably good side views available but the river was high when I was there
Notes: The bridge is the second longest single span covered bridge in Vermont. It re-opened to traffic inn 2004

World Index Number: VT/45-08-02
National Register of Historic Places: October 9, 1974

Gates Farm Covered Bridge (Little)
County: Lamoille, Vermont
Township: Cambridge

GPS Position: N 44° 38.741' W 72° 52.339'
Directions: From the town of Cambridge, take VT-15 northeast for about 0.3 miles and you will see the bridge on your right down a farm access road
Crosses: Seymour River
Carries: Farm road
Builder: Blow and Cote (Original George W. Holmes)
Year Built: 1995 (Original 1897) (M1950) (R1995)
Truss Type: Multiple King with Burr Arch
Dimensions: 1 Span, 82 Feet

Photo Tips: You can take photographs from the public road, but note that closer views take you onto private land
Notes: In 1950, the Seymour River course was changed and this bridge became unnecessary. The river course change separated the Gates farm from its fields and the bridge was moved to provide access to farm machinery

World Index Number: VT/45-08-04#2
National Register of Historic Places: Not Listed

Lumber Mill Covered Bridge (Lower)
County: Lamoille, Vermont
Township: Belvidere

GPS Position: N 44° 44.636' W 72° 44.476'
Directions: From Belivere Jucntion take Back Road north off VT-109 and you will find the bridge in about 0.5 miles
Crosses: North Branch of the Lamoille River
Carries: Back Road

Builder: Lewis Robinson
Year Built: 1895 (R1972) (R1995) (R2001)
Truss Type: Queen
Dimensions: 1 Span, 71 Feet

Photo Tips: Good views from all sides particularly a side view from the river bank
Notes: After a 1971 truck accident, steel beams and concrete abutments were added. It is located in a pleasant setting

World Index Number: VT/45-08-06
National Register of Historic Places: November 19, 1974

Morgan Covered Bridge (Upper)
County: Lamoille, Vermont
Township: Belvidere

GPS Position: N 44° 44.616' W 72° 43.684'
Directions: From Belvidere Junction go east on VT-109 for 0.8 miles and turn left on Morgan Bridge Road. The bridge is a short distance
Crosses: North Branch of the Lamoille River
Carries: Morgan Bridge Road

Builder: Lewis Robinson
Year Built: 1887 (R1898) (R2001)
Truss Type: Queen
Dimensions: 1 Span, 65 Feet

Photo Tips: Easy from all sides and from river level
Notes: Unlike nearby bridges, this one has not had steel beams added. Closed to traffic in 2005

World Index Number: VT/45-08-07
National Register of Historic Places: November 19, 1974

Power House CB (School St, Johnson)
County: Lamoille, Vermont
Township: Johnson

GPS Position: N 44° 38.161' W 72° 40.198'
Directions: From the town of Johnson take VT-100C northeast off VT-15/ Lower Main St. and the bridge is about 0.4 miles just left at School House Street
Crosses: Gihon River
Carries: School House Street

Builder: Not known
Year Built: 2002 (Original 1872) (R1960) (R1993)
Truss Type: Queen and King
Dimensions: 1 Span, 63 Feet

Photo Tips: Good views from all sides
Notes: The 2002 reconstruction was required because the original 1872 bridge collapsed under the weight of snow. The steel beams added in about 1995 were retained in the rebuilt structures
World Index Number: VT/45-08-08#2
National Register of Historic Places: Not listed

Scribner Covered Bridge (DeGosh)
County: Lamoille, Vermont
Township: Johnson

GPS Position: N 44° 38.278' W 72° 38.911'
Directions: From the town of East Johnson go east on VT-100C for 0.5 miles and turn right on Rocky Road. The bridge is found in about 0.3 miles
Crosses: Gihon River
Carries: Rocky Road

Builder: Not known
Year Built: Ca1919 (R1960)
Truss Type: Modified Queen
Dimensions: 1 Span, 48 Feet

Photo Tips: Easy from all sides
Notes: The bridge was uncovered until about 1919 when it was renovated as a covered bridge. In 1960 steel beams were added as well as cement abutments. It is a quiet setting.

World Index Number: VT/45-08-09
National Register of Historic Places: October 1, 1974

Red Covered Bridge (Sterling Brook, Chaffee)
County: Lamoille, Vermont
Township: Morriston

GPS Position: N 44° 31.109' W 72° 40.669'
Directions: From Morriston go east on Walton Rd and turn left onto Cole Rd after 0.7 miles. The bridge is about 3.9 miles
Crosses: Sterling Brook
Carries: Cole Road

Builder: Not known
Year Built: 1896 (R1897) (R1971) (R2002)
Truss Type: King and Queen with iron rods
Dimensions: 1 Span, 64 Feet

Photo Tips: Easy from all sides
Notes: Shortly after it was built it was twisted in a windstorm and iron rods were added to the truss system to strengthen it. A great looking bridge in a natural setting.
World Index Number: VT/45-08-11
National Register of Historic Places: October 16, 1974

Emily's CB (Stowe Hollow, Gold Brook)
County: Lamoille, Vermont
Township: Stowe

GPS Position: N 44° 26.422' W 72° 40.788'
Directions: From the town of Stowe go southeast on VT-108 for 1.1 miles and turn left on VT-100 and then the third right on School St. School St. becomes Stowe Hollow Rd., and then Covered Bridge Rd. and you will find the bridge site after about 2 miles
Crosses: Gold Brook
Carries: Covered Bridge Rd
Builder: John W. Smith
Year Built: 1844
Truss Type: Howe
Dimensions: 1 Span, 49 Feet
Photo Tips: There are nice tree shaded portal views as well as access to one side
Notes: The older name of Stowe Hollow Covered Bridge has been supplanted by Emily's Bridge and various tales of her haunting the bridge.

World Index Number: VT/45-08-12
National Register of Historic Places: October 1, 1974

Village Covered Bridge (Church St)
County: Lamoille, Vermont
Township: Waterville

GPS Position: N 44° 41.399' W 72° 46.262'
Directions: In the town of Waterville go east off VT-109 on Church Street and the bridge is a short distance
Crosses: North Branch of the Lamoille River
Carries: Church Street

Builder: Not known
Year Built: Ca1877 (R1968) (R2000)
Truss Type: Queen
Dimensions: 1 Span, 61 Feet

Photo Tips: Easy from all sides
Notes: The bridge was reinforced with steel beams in 1968 after a truck damaged it the previous year. Further truck damage caused its closing in 1999

World Index Number: VT/45-08-13
National Register of Historic Places: December 16, 1974

Montgomery Covered Bridge (Lower, Potter)
County: Lamoille, Vermont
Township: Waterville

GPS Position: N 44° 42.348' W 72° 45.616'
Directions: From Belvidere Junction go south on VT-109 for 2.3 miles and turn left onto Montgomery Road where you will see the bridge
Crosses: North Branch of the Lamoille River
Carries: Montgomery Road

Builder: Not known
Year Built: 1887 (R1969) (R1971) (R1997)
Truss Type: Queen
Dimensions: 1 Span, 70 Feet

Photo Tips: Easy from all sides and especially interesting from the rocks at the river
Notes: After problems with the snow load and then damage by a loaded truck, steel beams were added in 1971 to increase the load capacity

World Index Number: VT/45-08-14
National Register of Historic Places: October 18, 1974

Jaynes CB (Coddling Hollow, Upper)
County: Lamoille, Vermont
Township: Waterville

GPS Position: N 44° 42.719' W 72° 45.388'
Directions: From the town of Belvidere Junction go south on VT-109 for 1.8 miles and turn left on Codding Hollow Rd. The bridge is a short distance
Crosses: North Branch of the Lamoille River
Carries: Codding Hollow Rd.

Builder: Not known
Year Built: c1877 (R1960) (R2001)
Truss Type: Queenpost
Dimensions: 1 Span, 56 Feet

Photo Tips: Not an easy bridge to get a side view due to brush and shrubs
Notes: This bridge has had steel beams reinforcing it after a 1960 accident when a loaded truck fell through the floor

World Index Number: VT/45-08-06
National Register of Historic Places: October 1, 1974

Fisher Railroad Covered Bridge (Chubb)
County: Lamoille, Vermont
Township: Wolcot

GPS Position: N 44° 31.936' W 72° 25.660'
Directions: From the village of Potterville go east on VT-15 for 1.6 mile and you will see the bridge in a roadside park
Crosses: Lamoille River
Carries: Lamoille Valley Rail Trail (Abandoned Railroad Line)
Builder: St. Johnsbury and Lamoille County Railroad
Year Built: 1908
Truss Type: Town-Pratt
Dimensions: 1 Span, 98 Feet

Photo Tips: There are terrific shots available from the portal and sides and the truss system is interesting as well.
Notes: This is one of just 2 covered railroad bridges surviving in Vermont. It is a wonderful structure with an interesting cupola on the top which was used to vent smoke from the railway engine. The rail line is gone except a set of tracks through the building, which adds to the character

World Index Number: VT/45-08-16
National Register of Historic Places: October 1, 1974

Moxley Covered Bridge (Guy)
County: Orange , Vermont
Township: Chelsea

GPS Position: N 43° 57.436' W 72° 27.816'
Directions: From the town of North Turnbridge go north on VT-110 for 3.4 miles and turn right onto Moxley Rd. The bridge is a short distance
Crosses: First Branch of the White River
Carries: Moxley Rd

Builder: Arthur C. Adams
Year Built: 1883 (R2001)
Truss Type: Queen and King
Dimensions: 1 Span, 56 Feet

Photo Tips: Open on all sides
Notes: On a quiet road with hills in the background, it makes a pleasant stop. Its shape is actually not square as it is built to conform to the road which is angled to the river

World Index Number: VT/45-09-01
National Register of Historic Places: September 10, 1974

Kingsbury CB (Hyde, South Randolph)
County: Orange, Vermont
Township: Randolph

GPS Position: N 43° 52.850' W 72° 34.903'
Directions: From the village of East Randolph go south on VT-14 for 4.3 miles and turn right onto Kingsbury Rd where you will find the bridge
Crosses: Second Branch of the White River
Carries: Kingsbury Rd

Builder: Not known
Year Built: 1904 (R1958) (R1980) (R1994) (R2002)
Truss Type: Multiple Kingpost
Dimensions: 1 Span, 51 Feet

Photo Tips: Open on all sides
Notes: It looks in excellent condition, although vandalized by graffiti. It has no windows and is unpainted

World Index Number: VT/45-09-02
National Register of Historic Places: July 30, 1974

Gilford CB (C K Smith, Lower, Blue)
County: Orange, Vermont
Township: Randolph

GPS Position: N 43° 54.977' W 72° 33.330'
Directions: From East Randolph go south on VT-14 for 1.6 mi and turn right onto Hyde Rd where you will see the bridge
Crosses: South Branch of the White River
Carries: Hyde Road

Builder: Not known
Year Built: 1904 (R1985) (R2001) (R2011)
Truss Type: Multiple King
Dimensions: 1 Span, 54 Feet

Photo Tips: Open from all sides
Notes: This bridge has a lower and upper level of kingpost trusses and it has been suggested that it was once uncovered. It currently has a coat of orange-red paint and looks great

World Index Number: VT/45-09-03
National Register of Historic Places: July 30, 1974

Braley CB (Johnson, Upper, Blaisdell)
County: Orange, Vermont
Township: Randolph

GPS Position: N 43° 55.704' W 72° 33.337'
Directions: From East Randolph go south on VT-14 for 0.7 mi and turn right on Braley Rd. This road is sometimes called Blaisdell or Braley Covered Bridge Road. The bridge is about 0.3 miles
Crosses: Second Branch of White River
Carries: Braley Road
Builder: Not known
Year Built: 1904 (R1090) (R1977) (R2004)
Truss Type: Multiple Kingpost
Dimensions: 1 Span, 38 Feet

Photo Tips: Good side and front views
Notes: Originally built in 1883 as an uncovered box pony with kingpost, it was given another half height layer of multiple kingposts when roofed in 1904. The only other bridge like this is nearby Guilford Covered Bridge.

World Index Number: VT/45-09-04
National Register of Historic Places: June 13, 1974

Union Village Covered Bridge
County: Orange, Vermont
Township: Thetford

GPS Position: N 43° 47.321' W 72° 15.223'
Directions: From the village of Thetford Hill go south on Academy Rd off of VT-113 and the bridge is about 2.7 miles
Crosses: Ompompanoosuc River
Carries: Academy Rd

Builder: Not known
Year Built: (R1970) (R2002)
Truss Type: Multiple King Variation
Dimensions: 1 Span, 111 Feet

Photo Tips: Easy from all sides
Notes: It is essential a multiple Kingpost truss system with the addition of two long diagonals which may act as an arch. The ceiling trusses are also massive and interesting. The three large windows provide a nice balanced look

World Index Number: VT/45-09-05
National Register of Historic Places: September 17, 1974

Thetford Center Covered Bridge (Sayre)
County: Orange, Vermont
Township: Thetford

GPS Position: N 43° 49.939' W 72° 15.149'
Directions: From Thetford Center go north on VT-113 for 0.3 mi and turn left on Tucker Hill Rd. The bridge is found in a short distance.
Crosses: Ompompanoosuc River
Carries: Tucker Hill Road

Builder: Not known
Year Built: 1839 (R1963) (R1997) (R2007)
Truss Type: Haupt (or Burr variation)
Dimensions: 1 span (later center pier added), 127 Feet

Photo Tips: Front and side setups are available
Notes: In 1963 the center concrete pier was added to allow for heavier traffic load. The 1997 repairs were required after a truck truck attempted to drive through with its bed raised, destroying part of the ceiling supports.

World Index Number: VT/45-09-06
National Register of Historic Places: September 17, 1974

Howe Covered Bridge
County: Orange, Vermont
Township: Tunbridge

GPS Position: N 43° 51.890' W 72° 29.901'
Directions: From Tunbridge go south on VT-110 for 3 mi and turn left on Belknap Brook Rd where you will see the bridge
Crosses: First Branch of the White River
Carries: Belknap Brook Rd

Builder: Ira Mudget, Edward Wells and Chauncey Tenney
Year Built: 1879 (R1994) (R2002)
Truss Type: Multiple King
Dimensions: 1 Span, 75 Feet

Photo Tips: Views from all sides but a bit of shrubs on the side views
Notes: The Kingpost also have vertical bars through the diagonal members. There is an old homemade ladder kept on one interior wall which apparently is there by long tradition rather than any current use

World Index Number: VT/45-09-07
National Register of Historic Places: September 10, 1974

Cilley Covered Bridge (Lower)
County: Orange, Vermont
Township: Tunbridge

GPS Position: N 43° 52.977' W 72° 30.256'
Directions: From Tunbridge go south on VT-100 for about 1.5 mi and turn right onto Howe Lane. The bridge is about 0.2 mi
Crosses: First Branch of the White River
Carries: Howe Lane

Builder: Arthur C. Adams
Year Built: 1883 (R2002) (R2006)
Truss Type: Multiple Kingpost
Dimensions: 1 Span, 68 Feet

Photo Tips: Easy from all sides
Notes: Found in a quiet setting, it has low hills behind to set it off

World Index Number: VT/45-09-08
National Register of Historic Places: September 10, 1974

Hayward Covered Bridge (Noble, Mill)
County: Orange, Vermont
Township: Tunbridge

GPS Position: N 43° 53.485' W 72° 29.486'
Directions: In Tunbridge, the bridge is just north on Spring Rd
Crosses: First Branch of White River
Carries: Spring Road

Builder: Neil Daniels Construction (Original Arthur C. Adams)
Year Built: 2000 (Original 1883)
Truss Type: Multiple King
Dimensions: 1 Span, 72 Feet

Photo Tips: There is a good side view from the east side of spring road on the north end of the bridge but be careful of traffic
Notes: The original structure was destroyed by an ice jam in 1999 and replaced by the current authentic structure the next year

World Index Number: VT/45-09-09#2
National Register of Historic Places: Not Listed

Larkin Covered Bridge
County: Orange, Vermont
Township: Tunbridge

GPS Position: N 43° 55.381' W 72° 27.894'
Directions: From Tunbridge go north on VT-110 for 2 miles and turn right onto Larkin Road. The bridge is a short distance
Crosses: First Branch of the White River
Carries: Larkin Road

Builder: Arthur C. Adams
Year Built: 1902 (R2002)
Truss Type: Multiple Kingpost
Dimensions: 1 Span, 68 Feet

Photo Tips: Easily seen from all sides
Notes: It can be seen from the main Highway VT-110. It is in a quiet setting and makes a pleasant visit

World Index Number: VT/45-09-10
National Register of Historic Places: July 30,1974

Flint Covered Bridge
County: Orange, Vermont
Township: Tunbridge

GPS Position: N 43° 56.956' W 72° 27.495'
Directions: From Tunbridge go north on VT-110 for 3.9 mi and turn right on Bicknell Hill Rd. The bridge is a short distance
Crosses: First Branch of the White River
Carries: Bicknell Hill Road

Builder: Not known
Year Built: 1874 (R1969) (R2002)
Truss Type: King and Queen
Dimensions: 1 Span, 87 Feet

Photo Tips: Easy from all sides
Notes: The oldest of the Tunbridge area bridges, it is a peaceful place to stop for a visit

World Index Number: VT/45-09-11
National Register of Historic Places: September 10, 1974

Lords Creek Covered Bridge
County: Orleans, Vermont
Township: Irasburg

GPS Position: N 44° 48.993' W 72° 15.971'
Directions: From Orleans, take VT-58 west for 2.7 miles and turn right onto Covered Bridge Rd. The bridge is about 1.2 mi
Crosses: Black River
Carries: Covered Bridge Road

Builder: John D. Colton
Year Built: 1881 (M1958)
Truss Type: Paddleford
Dimensions: 1 Span, 50 Feet

Photo Tips: Easy from all sides.
Notes: Moved in 1958 and now on private road as access to farm

World Index Number: VT/45-10-01
National Register of Historic Places: Not listed

Orne Covered Bridge (Coventry, Lower)
County: Orleans, Vermont
Township: Irasburg

GPS Position: N 44° 51.641' W 72° 16.444'
Directions: From Coventry go west on Main St. off US-5 and after0.5 miles, a slight right onto Covered Bridge Road. The bridge is about 0.5 miles along this road
Crosses: Black River
Carries: Covered Bridge Road

Builder: Original bridge built by J.D. Colton
Year Built: 1999 (Original 1881)
Truss Type: Paddleford
Dimensions: 1 Span, 87 Feet

Photo Tips: Easy from all sides
Notes: The original bridge was arsoned in 1997 and replaced with this near replica authentic bridge in 1999. It is one of a small number of surviving bridges using the Paddleford Truss system

World Index Number: VT/45-10-02#2
National Register of Historic Places: Not listed

Sanderson Covered Bridge
County: Rutland, Vermont
Township: Brandon

GPS Position: N 43° 47.367' W 73° 06.686'
Directions: From Brandon go south on Pearl Street off US-7.
The bridge is 1.2 miles
Crosses: Otter Creek
Carries: Pearl Street

Builder: Blow and Cote
Year Built: 2003 (Original 1840)
Truss Type: Town
Dimensions: 1 Span, 132 Feet

Photo Tips: Easy from all sides
Notes: The original bridge was closed to vehicles and the
rebuilt bridge was completed in 2003 allowing traffic to reopen.
Some of the original bridge structure was used in the rebuild.

World Index Number: VT/45-11-02#2
National Register of Historic Places: Not listed

Kingsley Covered Bridge (Mill River)
County: Rutland, Vermont
Township: Clarendon

GPS Position: N 43° 31.418' W 72° 56.459'
Directions: From Cuttingsville take VT-103 northwest for 3.4 mi and turn left on Airport Rd, continuing on Gorge Rd/ River Rd. After 0.5 miles, turn left on East St. and the bridge is just ahead
Crosses: Mill River
Carries: State Route 1020/Winding Road
Builder: Timothy Horton
Year Built: 1836 (R1870) (R1950) (R1985) (R1999) (R2002)
Truss Type: Town
Dimensions: 1 Span, 121 Feet

Photo Tips: There are good views near the mill if the water is not too high
Notes: If the 1836 build date is correct, this is one of the oldest bridges in North America. Some claims say the 1870 repair was in fact a replacement. The restored Kingsley Mill is nearby.

World Index Number: VT/45-11-03
National Register of Historic Places: February 12, 1974

Gorham Covered Bridge (Goodnough)
County: Rutland, Vermont
Township: Pittsford

GPS Position: N 43° 40.798' W 73° 02.237'
Directions: Take VT-3/ Corn Hill Rd. south from Us-7 east of Pittsford for 2 miles and then make a right on Gorham Bridge Rd. The bridge is about 0.4 miles
Crosses: Otter Creek
Carries: Esther Furnace Road

Builder: Contractors Crane Service (Original Nichols Powers)
Year Built: 2004 (Original 1842)
Truss Type: Town
Dimensions: 1 Span, 115 Feet

Photo Tips: Excellent open looks from all sides
Notes: This historically authentic bridge replaced the original built in 1842. Nichols Powers, one of the most famous of bridge builders, was Abraham Owen's apprentice but by the 1840s when the original was built, he had become his partner

World Index Number: VT/45-11-04#2
National Register of Historic Places: Not listed

Hammond Covered Bridge
County: Rutland, Vermont
Township: Pittsford

GPS Position: N 43° 43.238' W 73° 03.239'
Directions: From the town of Pittsford, go northwest on US-7/ Franklin St. for 1 mile and turn left on Kendall Hill Road. The bridge site is about 0.8 miles
Crosses: Otter Creek
Carries: Kendall Hill Road

Builder: Asa Nourse
Year Built: 1842 (R1927) (R2005)
Truss Type: Town
Dimensions: 1 Span, 139 Feet

Photo Tips: Easy from all sides
Notes: This is a great looking bridge in a quiet natural setting. Like many of the covered bridges at risk from the large flood of 1927, it suffered damage and was washed more than a mile downstream. It was floated back on barrels and replaced

World Index Number: VT/45-11-05
National Register of Historic Places: January 21, 1974

Depot Covered Bridge
County: Rutland, Vermont
Township: Pittsford

GPS Position: N 43° 42.577' W 73° 02.557'
Directions: From Pittsford, go northwest on US-7 for 0.2 miles and turn right on Depot Hill Rd. The bridge is found in about 0.8 miles
Crosses: Otter Creek
Carries: Depot Hill Rd
Builder: Abraham Owen
Year Built: 1853 (R1974) (R1985) (R2005)
Truss Type: Town
Dimensions: 1 Span, 121 Feet

Photo Tips: Good easy views from all sides
Notes: It is quiet now but at one time it was near an active railroad station and from that it took its name. From the images, you can see that railway ties have been placed on a diagonal to stabilize the structure from wind, something that the Town Truss has a weakness to

World Index Number: VT/45-11-06
National Register of Historic Places: January 21, 1974

Cooley Covered Bridge
County: Rutland, Vermont
Township: Pittsford

GPS Position: N 43° 41.427' W 73° 01.691'
Directions: From the town of Pittsford, go south off of US-7 on Elm St. You will find the bridge site in a about 1 mile
Crosses: Furnace Brook
Carries: Elm St.

Builder: Nichols Montgomery Powers
Year Built: 1849 (R2004)
Truss Type: Town
Dimensions: 1 Span, 51 feet

Photo Tips: This is a beautiful little bridge and looks terrific in its coat of barn red paint. Easy from all sides.
Notes: This bridge has been likened to a stranded Conestoga Wagon which it certainly resembles. The bridge is named after Benjamin Cooley, an early settler to the area and soldier in the Revolutionary War

World Index Number: VT/45-11-07
National Register of Historic Places: January 24, 1974

Brown Covered Bridge (Hollow)
County: Rutland, Vermont
Township: Shrewsbury

GPS Position: N 43° 33.962' W 72° 55.107'
Directions: From North Clarendon, take Shrewsbury Rd. east off US-4 and continue on Cold River Rd. In 2.4 miles, go left on Upper Cold River Rd and the bridge is a short distance
Crosses: Cold River
Carries: Upper Cold River Rd

Builder: Nichols Montgomery Powers
Year Built: 1880 (R2002) (R2015)
Truss Type: Town
Dimensions: 1 Span, 112 feet

Photo Tips: It is in a hollow and you might want to plan on using a tripod, as it can be dark
Notes: This is the last bridge built by Nichols Powers when he was in his early sixties. It is one of his finest structures

World Index Number: VT/45-11-09
National Register of Historic Places: January 21, 1974

Coburn Covered Bridge (Cemetery)
County: Washington, Vermont
Township: East Montpelier

GPS Position: N 44° 16.855' W 72° 27.233'
Directions: From the town of North Montpelier, go south on VT-14 for 0.8 miles and turn left on Coburn Road. After about 1 mile you will reach the bridge site
Crosses: Winooski River
Carries: Coburn Road
Builder: Larned Coburn
Year Built: 1851 (R1961) (R1973) (R1997)
Truss Type: Queen and King
Dimensions: 1 Span, 69 feet

Photo Tips: Excellent portal plus side views from river level
Notes: This bridge is currently unpainted which is apparently the original state of historic covered bridges. The builder, Larned Coburn, wanted the main road to be re-routed to go by his property and offered to build the bridge if it was. This offer was accepted

World Index Number: VT/45-12-02
National Register of Historic Places: October 9, 1974

Martin Covered Bridge (Orton Farm, Orton)
County: Washington, Vermont
Township: Marshfield

GPS Position: N 44° 17.255' W 72° 24.543'
Directions: From North Montpelier go south on VT-214 for 1.9 miles and then turn left on US-2. The bridge is 1.6 miles.
Crosses: Winooski River
Carries: Farm road

Builder: Herman F. Townsend
Year Built: 1890 (M2004) (R2009)
Truss Type: Queen
Dimensions: 1 Span, 45 Feet

Photo Tips: Easy from all sides
Notes: The bridge was moved to its present site after the town of Marshfield obtained it and the surrounding land in lieu of outstanding taxes. It is an excellent spot for a family outing and picnic

World Index Number: VT45-12-06
National Register of Historic Places: October 9, 1974

Moseley Covered Bridge (Stony Brook)
County: Washington, Vermont
Township: Northfield

GPS Position: N 44° 07.709' W 72° 41.775'
Directions: From Northfield take VT-12A south for 1.5 mi and turn right onto Stoney Brook Rd. The bridge is about 1.5 mi
Crosses: Stoney Brook
Carries: Stoney Brook Road

Builder: John Moseley
Year Built: 1899 (R1971) (R1978) (R1990)
Truss Type: King
Dimensions: 1 Span, 37 Feet

Photo Tips: Access to the sides is a bit obscured by brush
Notes: Steel beams were added in 1971. The kingpost trusses are only part way up the sides but sufficient for a short span like this. It is unusual in being painted inside as well as out

World Index Number: VT/45-12-07
National Register of Historic Places: November 20, 1974

Station Covered Bridge (Northfield Falls)
County: Washington, Vermont
Township: Northfield

GPS Position: N 44° 10.351' W 72° 39.084'
Directions: In the town of Northfield Falls the bridge is on Cox Brook Road just west of the intersection with VT-12
Crosses: Dog River
Carries: Cox Brook Road

Builder: Not known
Year Built: 1872 (R1963) (R1978) (R1993) (R2002)
Truss Type: Town
Dimensions:1+ Span (Center pier added in 1963), 137 Feet

Photo Tips: Side views are difficult and you need to be careful of traffic. You can get two bridges in the same image, this one and the Second Covered Bridge
Notes: As well as having a pier added in 1963 it also had steel beams placed. It has two other bridges in the vicinity, Second and Third Covered Bridges, all three of which are painted red

World Index Number: VT/45-12-08
National Register of Historic Places: August 13, 1974

Slaughter House Covered Bridge
County: Washington, Vermont
Township: Northfield

GPS Position: N 44° 10.112' W 72° 39.268'
Directions: Fom the Town of Northfield Falls go east of VT-12 on Slaughter House Road. The bridge is a short distance
Crosses: Dog River
Carries: Slaughter House Road

Builder: Not known
Year Built: 1872 (R1978() (R2002)
Truss Type: Queenpost
Dimensions: 1 Span, 60 Feet

Photo Tips: You can, with care, get to the river bank for side views
Notes: Like the other area bridges, steel beams were added to strengthen it. The portals are rounded unlike other Vermont bridges

World Index Number: VT/45-12-09
National Register of Historic Places: June 13, 1974

Second CB (Lower, Cox Brook, Newell)
County: Washington, Vermont
Township: Northfield

GPS Position: N 44° 10.366' W 72° 39.151'
Directions: In the town of Northfield Falls go east off of VT-12 on Cox Brook Road, to the second covered bridge. The first is the Station Covered Bridge
Crosses: Cox Brook
Carries: Cox Brook Road

Builder: Not known
Year Built: 1872 (R1960) (R1978)
Truss Type: Queenpost
Dimensions: 1 Span, 57 Feet

Photo Tips: You can get this bridge and Station in the same image
Notes: One of three covered bridges on this road with Station and Third Bridge. All are painted barn red

World Index Number: VT/45-12-10
National Register of Historic Places: October 15, 1974

Third Covered Bridge (Upper Cox Brook)
County: Washington, Vermont
Township: Northfield

GPS Position: N 44° 10.425' W 72° 39.337'
Directions: In the town of Northfield Falls go east off of VT-12 on Cox Brook Road, to the third covered bridge, about 0.3 miles. The first two are the Station Covered Bridge and Second Covered Bridge.
Crosses: Cox Brook
Carries: Cox Brook Road

Builder: Not known
Year Built: Ca1872 (R1966) (R1978) (R2002)
Truss Type: Queenpost
Dimensions: 1 Span, 52 Feet

Photo Tips: You can with care get side views
Notes: One of three covered bridges on this road with Station and Second Bridge. All are painted barn red

World Index Number: VT/45-12-11
National Register of Historic Places: October 1, 1974

Pine Brook Covered Bridge (Wilder)
County: Washington, Vermont
Township: Waitsfield

GPS Position: N 44° 12.339' W 72° 47.549'
Directions: From Waitsfield take VT-100 north for 1.4 miles and turn right onto Trembly Rd and then after 0.8 miles, left onto North Road. The bridge is then a short distance
Crosses: Pine Brook
Carries: North Road

Builder: Not known
Year Built: 1872 (R1977) (R1989) (R2001)
Truss Type: Kingpost
Dimensions: 1 Span, 48 Feet

Photo Tips: Easy from all sides, and good long views
Notes: In this quiet country setting, it would be easy to expect to see a horse and carriage to pass through this bridge. It was renovated by Milton Gratton in 1977

World Index Number: VT/45-12-12
National Register of Historic Places: June 13, 1974

Big Eddy CB (Village, Great Eddy)
County: Washington, Vermont
Township: Waitsfield

GPS Position: N 44° 11.362' W 72° 49.409'
Directions: Found in the town of Waitsfield on Bridge St. just east of VT-100
Crosses: Mad River
Carries: Bridge St

Builder: Not known
Year Built: 1833 (R1940)
Truss Type: Multiple Kingpost with Burr Arch
Dimensions: 1 Span, 105 Feet

Photo Tips: The portal views can have a lot of traffic, good side views from the river bank
Notes: Vermont's second oldest bridge, the walkway was added about 1940

World Index Number: VT/45-12-14
National Register of Historic Places: September 6, 1974

Warren Covered Bridge (Lincoln Gap)
County: Washington, Vermont
Township: Warren

GPS Position: N 44° 06.672' W 72° 51.411'
Directions: Found in the town of Warren on the Warren Bridge Road just east of Town Highway 44
Crosses: Mad River
Carries: Warren Bridge Road

Builder: Walter Bagley
Year Built: 1880 (R1995) (R2000) (R2013)
Truss Type: Queen
Dimensions: 1 Span, 55 Feet

Photo Tips: Easy from all sides
Notes: The bridge was closed in 1998 for a major restoration and re-opened to traffic in 2000. It originally had an asymmetrical portal design but this was corrected in 2000

World Index Number: VT/45-12-15
National Register of Historic Places: August 7, 1974

Robbins Nest Covered Bridge
County: Washington, Vermont
Township: Barre

GPS Position: N 44° 10.735' W 72° 28.261'
Directions: From the town of Barre take Washington St./ VT-302 southeast continuing on Eat Barre Road and after 1.3 miles, you will see the bridge on the right on a private road
Crosses: Branch of Stevens Brook
Carries: Private Road
Builder: Robert R. Robbins
Year Built: 1964 (R1990) (R1993)
Truss Type: Queen
Dimensions: 1 Span, 57 Feet

Photo Tips: The bridge is on private property but it is easy to get images from the public roadside. Be careful as it has a lot of traffic
Notes: The bridge is a private project which is a replica of a bridge washed away in a flood in 1927 which had been located nearby. Steel beams were added in 1990

World Index Number: VT/45-12-18
National Register of Historic Places: Not listed

A.M. Foster Covered Bridge
County: Washington, Vermont
Township: Cabot

GPS Position: N 44° 25.416' W 72° 16.042'
Directions: From Cabot, go northeast on Route 215 for 1.3 miles and turn right onto Cabot Plains Rd. After 1.6 miles, you will see the bridge in a field on your right
Crosses: Pond
Carries: Pedestrian walkway

Builder: Richard Spaulding, Douglas Blondine, Frank Foster
Year Built: 1988
Truss Type: Queenpost
Dimensions: 1 Span, 57 feet

Photo Tips: There are wide views from all sides with a millpond to offer reflections. It is on private property
Notes: It was designed after the the Martin Covered Bridge which still stands near Marshfield. It was named after the great-grandfather of one of the builders

World Index Number: VT/45-12-75
National Register of Historic Places: Not listed

Creamery Covered Bridge (Centreville)
County: Windham, Vermont
Township: Brattleboro

GPS Position: N 42° 51.012' W 72° 35.119'
Directions: From I-91 north of Guilford, take Exit 2 onto VT-9 going west. After 0.3 miles turn left on Guildford St. and you will see the bridge
Crosses: Whetstone River
Carries: Guildford St.
Builder: A. H. Wright
Year Built: 1879 (R1917) (R2007)
Truss Type: Town
Dimensions: 1 Span, 80 Feet

Photo Tips: In the fall, there is a nice side view with colorful sumac in the foreground. Be careful of traffic, it can be busy
Notes: This is the only bridge known to have a slate roof which was added in 1917. At one time it was highly decorated at Christmas including Santa and reindeer on the roof. it replaced a bridge washed away in a 1878 flood

World Index Number: VT/45-13-01
National Register of Historic Places: August 28, 1973

West Dummerston Covered Bridge
County: Windham, Vermont
Township: Dummerston

GPS Position: N 42° 56.170' W 72° 36.777'
Directions: From of Brattleboro go north on VT-30 for 5.78 mi and turn right on West Dummerston Covered Bridge Rd where you will see the bridge
Crosses: West River
Carries: West Dummerston Covered Bridge Road

Builder: Renaud Brothers (Original Caleb Lamson)
Year Built: 1998 (Original 1872) (R1995)
Truss Type: Town
Dimensions: 2 Spans, 280 Feet

Photo Tips: There are great views from all sides. Look especially for a long side view from the south
Notes: This is one of the finest bridges in Vermont and it is in a great setting, particularly beautiful in the fall

World Index Number: VT/45-13-02#2
National Register of Historic Places: Not listed

Kidder Hill Covered Bridge
County: Windham, Vermont
Township: Grafton

GPS Position: N 43° 10.119' W 72° 36.333'
Directions: From the town of Grafton, go south off VT-121/ Main St. on Kidder Hill Rd. and the bridge is 0.2 miles
Crosses: South Branch of Saxton's River
Carries: Kidder Hill Road

Builder: Not known
Year Built: 1870 (R1950) (R1995)
Truss Type: Kingpost
Dimensions: 1 Span, 67 Feet

Photo Tips: There are great side views from the river level which is easy to get to
Notes: This bridge replaced a bridge destroyed in an 1869 flood. It is the longest of Vermont's Kingpost trussed bridges

World Index Number: VT/45-13-03
National Register of Historic Places: July 2, 1973

Green River Covered Bridge
Township: Guilford, Vermont
County: Windham

GPS Position: N 42° 46.531' W 72° 40.018'
Directions: From I-91 just north of Guilford, take Exit 1 south on US-5 and go 1.4 miles where you turn right on Guilford Center Rd. After 4.6 miles turn right on Jacksonville Stage Rd and the bridge site is about 2.4 miles
Crosses: Green River
Carries: Jacksonville Stage Rd
Builder: Marcus Worden
Year Built: 1870 (R2014) (R2016)
Truss Type: Town
Dimensions: 1 Span, 104 Feet
Photo Tips: This is a great looking bridge and you will have no problem finding good views from all sides
Notes: Just downstream from a dam, the Green River Covered bridge is an elegant structure with barn red portals set against its unpainted weathered sides. Up until 2001, the bridge housed local mailboxes

World Index Number: VT/45-13-04
National Register of Historic Places: August 28, 1973

Williamsville Covered Bridge
County: Windham, Vermont
Township: Newfane

GPS Position: N 42° 56.653' W 72° 44.306'
Directions: From the town of East Dover go east on Dover Hill Road for 2.4 miles where you will find the bridge
Crosses: Rock River
Carries: Dover Hill Road

Builder: Alpine Construction (Original Eugene F. Wheller)
Year Built: 2010 (Original 1869) (R1950) (R1980) (R1990)
Truss Type: Town
Dimensions: 1 Span, 118 Feet

Photo Tips: There are views from all sides
Notes: Found in a natural setting and a spectacular one during the height of fall foliage

World Index Number: VT/45-13-05#2
National Register of Historic Places: Not listed

Hall Covered Bridge (Park, Osgood)
County: **Windham , Vermont**
Township: **Rockingham**

GPS Position: N 43° 08.210' W 72° 29.267'
Directions: From Saxtons River, go east on VT-121 for 1 mile and turn left on Hall Bridge Rd. where you will see the bridge
Crosses: Saxton's River
Carries: Hall Bridge Rd

Builder: Milton Graton (Original Eugene P. Wheeler)
Year Built: 1982 (Original 1870)
Truss Type: Town
Dimensions: 1 Span, 121 Feet

Photo Tips: There are excellent side views which include the diamond shaped windows
Notes: An overloaded truck damaged the original bridge in 1980, and the replacement was completed in 1982 by Milton Graton who used a team of oxen to haul the bridge into place.

World Index Number: VT/45-13-07#2
National Register of Historic Places: Not listed

Worrall Covered Bridge
County: Windham, Vermont
Township: Rockingham

GPS Position: N 43° 12.702' W 72° 32.127'
Directions: From Rockingham take VT-103 northeast for 3.4 miles and turn right onto Williams Road. The bridge is a short distance
Crosses: William's River
Carries: Williams Road

Builder: Cold River Bridges (Original Sanford Granger)
Year Built: 2012 (Original 1868)
Truss Type: Town
Dimensions: 1 Span, 83 Feet

Photo Tips: Easy from all sides
Notes: In the fall of 2009, this bridge was under repairs. It also suffered from flood damage from Hurricane Irene in August of 2011

World Index Number: TN/45-13-10
National Register of Historic Places: July 16, 1973

Bartonsville Covered Bridge
County: Windham, Vermont
Township: Rockingham

GPS Position: N 43° 13.445' W 72° 32.230'
Directions: from the town of Rockingham, take VT-103/Rockingham Rd east for 4.5 miles and turn right onto Lower Bartonsville Rd. The bridge is about 0.3 miles on the right
Crosses: Williams River
Carries: Lower Bartonsville Rd

Builder: Cold River Bridges
Year Built: 2012 (Original 1870)
Truss Type: Town
Dimensions: 1 Span, 168 feet

Photo Tips: Easy from all sides
Notes: The original 1870 bridge was destroyed by Hurricane Irene in 2011. The rebuild was finished in 2012 and officially opened in January, 2013.

World Index Number: VT/45-13-11#2
National Register of Historic Places: September 17, 1980

Scott Covered Bridge
County: Windham, Vermont
Township: Townsend

GPS Position: N 43° 02.930' W 72° 41.789'
Directions: From the town of Townshend go east of VT-30 for 1.5 miles and the bridge will be on your left
Crosses: West River
Carries: Scott Bridge Road (Bypassed)
Builder: Harrison Chamberlin
Year Built: 1870
Truss Type: Town and King with Burr Arch
Dimensions: 3 Spans, 276 Feet

Photo Tips: One of Vermont's great bridges, it can be viewed from all sides including well as good long side views
Notes: Although built in 1870, it wasn't covered until 1873. A concrete pier was added in 1981. The different spans were built as seperate units , so the structure is actually three bridges joined. The Town truss section is the longest span in Vermont at 166 feet. It was closed to traffic in 1955

World Index Number: VT/45-13-13
National Register of Historic Places: August 28, 1973

Victorian Village Covered Bridge (Depot)
County: Windham, Vermont
Township: Rockingham

GPS Position: N 43° 11.680' W 72° 30.079'
Directions: From the town of Rockingham go northwest on VT-103 for 0.8 miles until you see the Vermont Country Store on the left. The bridge is on their property
Crosses: Rock Brook
Carries: Pedestrian walkway
Builder: Aubrey Stratton (Original Sanford Grangers
Year Built: 1967 (Original 1872) (M1859)
Truss Type: King
Dimensions: 1 Span, 44 Feet

Photo Tips: Easy from all sides. Note the nearby gristmill as well
Notes: The bridge was originally built in Townshend, Vermont and was dismantled in 1959 by the Army Corps of Engineers when the area was to be flooded. It was rebuilt as a shorter bridge with Kingpost trusses in 1967 at its current location

World Index Number: VT/45-13-23
National Register of Historic Places: Not listed

Martinsville Covered Bridge (Martin's Mill)
County: Windsor, Vermont
Township: Hartland

GPS Position: N 43° 31.955' W 72° 23.749'
Directions: From the town of Hartland, take US-5 east and after 0.4 miles turn right on Depot Rd and then another quick right onto Martinsville Rd. The bridge site is about 0.7 miles
Crosses: Lull's Brook
Carries: Martinsville Rd

Builder: James F. Tasker
Year Built: 1881 (R1979)
Truss Type: Town
Dimensions: 1 Span, 135 Feet

Photo Tips: While not a particularly photogenic structure, it is easy to find clear set up areas
Notes: The ruins of the old mill are near the bridge. The area is quiet now but once had a busy industrial operation

World Index Number: VT/45-14-01
National Register of Historic Places: August 28, 1973

Willard CB (North Hartland, East Twin)
County: Windsor, Vermont
Township: Hartland

GPS Position: N 43° 35.611' W 72° 20.973'
Directions: From the town of North Hartland take Ewarts Drts Drive south off US-5 and take the first left on Mill St. The bridge is then a short distance
Crosses: Ottauquechee River
Carries: Mill St
Builder: Not Known
Year Built: 1870 (R1953) (R1979)
Truss Type: Town
Dimensions: 1 Span, 124 Feet

Photo Tips: It is easy to get a shot with both bridges in the frame. Side views are available with care
Notes: The bridge originally was without windows which were added in the 1953 renovation. This was said to keep horses from being startled by the rough water below. Just west of this bridge is another called the Williard Twin Covered Bridge

World Index Number: VT/45-14-02
National Register of Historic Places: August 28, 1973

Baltimore Covered Bridge
County: Windsor, Vermont
Township: Springfield

GPS Position: N 43° 16.240' W 72° 26.877'
Directions: From I-91, take exit 7,6 miles north of Rockingham, and continue on Charleston Rd./ VT-11 for 1.2 miles where you will see the bridge on your right
Crosses: Unnamed creek
Carries: None
Builder: Granville Leland
Year Built: 1870 (M1970) (R1970)
Truss Type: Town
Dimensions: 1 Span, 45 feet
Photo Tips: There are good images available from three sides and in the fall, it is fronted by a colorful stand of sumac
Notes: This bridge was relocated in 1970 and restored by Milton Grafton. It was formerly located in North Springfield over Great Brook. The historic Eureka Schoolhouse is beside it.

World Index Number: VT/45-14-03
National Register of Historic Places: Not listed

Titcomb Covered Bridge (Stoughton)
County: Windsor, Vermont
Township: Weathersfield

GPS Position: N 43° 22.131' W 72° 31.056'
Directions: Found at the south end of the town of Perkinsville on Highway VT-106. It can be seen from the road in a field across from the Weathersfield Elementary School
Crosses: Schoolhouse Brook
Carries: Private lane

Builder: James F. Taskar
Year Built: 1880 (M1959) (R1963)
Truss Type: Multiple Kingpost
Dimensions: 1 Span, 45 Feet

Photo Tips: Easy from all sides as the landowner allows visitors
Notes: This bridge was originally located across the North Branch of the Black River in Perkinsville. It was moved to its present location due to the construction of a reservoir in 1950

World Index Number: VT/45-14-04
National Register of Historic Places: Not listed

Salmond Covered Bridge
County: Windsor, Vermont
Township: Weathersfield

GPS Position: N 43° 25.626' W 72° 29.285'
Directions: From the town of Cavendish go northeast on VT-131 and after 9 miles, turn left on Henry Gould Rd. The bridge is a short distance along this road
Crosses: Sherman Brook
Carries: Henry Gould Rd.
Builder: James F. Tasker
Year Built: c1875 (M1959) (M1986) (R1986) (R2002)
Truss Type: Multiple King
Dimensions: 1 Span, 53 Feet

Photo Tips: Easy from all sides and you can have a picnic
Notes: This bridge was originally located near Stoughton Pond and crossed the Black River. It was moved when a reservoir was being built in that area and was used as a storage shed. In 1986 it was restored to use as a bridge when it was moved to its present site

World Index Number: VT/45-14-05
National Register of Historic Places: June 22, 1979

Upper Falls Covered Bridge (Downer's)
County: Windsor, Vermont
Township: Weathersfield

GPS Position: N 43° 23.893' W 72° 31.337'
Directions: From the village of Greenbush, go south on VT-6 for 1.2 miles and turn right onto VT-131 and after 0.3 miles, turn left onto Upper Falls Road. The bridge is a short distance
Crosses: Black River
Carries: Upper Falls Road

Builder: James F. Tasker
Year Built: c1840 (R1976)
Truss Type: Town
Dimensions: 1 Span, 120 Feet

Photo Tips: Great views from all sides, including side views at river level.
Notes: The great looking stone abutments have concrete caps used to raise the structure during the 1976 renovation. A nice spot for a family visit and picnic

World Index Number: VT/45-14-08
National Register of Historic Places: August 28, 1973

Best's Covered Bridge (Swallows)
County: Windsor, Vermont
Township: West Windsor

GPS Position: N 43° 27.300' W 72° 30.986'
Directions: From the town of Fletchville, take VT-106 north for 1 mile and turn right onto VT-44. After 1.5 miles turn right onto Churchill Road and the bridge is just ahead of you
Crosses: Mill Brook
Carries: Churchill Road

Builder: A. W. Swallows
Year Built: 1889 (R1973) (R1991)
Truss Type: Tied Arch
Dimensions: 1 Span, 37 Feet

Photo Tips: Easy all sides
Notes: A very simple looking windowless structure but have a look at the tied arch which is interesting

World Index Number: VT/45-14-10
National Register of Historic Places: July 2, 1973

Bower's Covered Bridge (Brownsville)
County: Windsor, Vermont
Township: West Windsor

GPS Position: N 43° 27.662' W 72° 29.438'
Directions: From the town of Brownsville take VT-44 southwest for 1.3 miles, then right on Bible Hill Rd and right on Bowers Rd.
Crosses: Mill Brook
Carries: Bowers Road

Builder: Not known
Year Built: c1919 (R2001) (R2012)
Truss Type: Tied Arch
Dimensions: 1 Span, 45 Feet

Photo Tips: Easy from all sides
Notes: As seen in the above photograph the bridge was rebuilt in 2012 after damage to the abutments from Hurricane Irene, Uses the interesting Tied Arch

World Index Number: VT/45-14-11
National Register of Historic Places: August 28, 1973

Taftsville Covered Bridge
County: Windsor, Vermont
Township: Woodstock

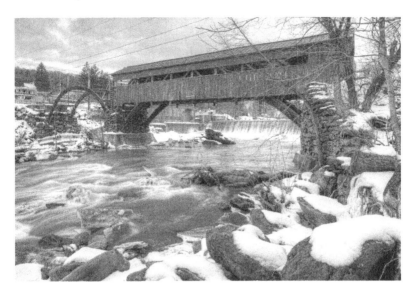

GPS Position: N 43° 37.866' W 72° 28.058'
Directions: From the town of Taftsville, take River Road north off of US-4/VT-12 and the bridge is a short distance
Crosses: Ottauquechee River
Carries: River Road
Builder: Solomon Emmons III
Year Built: 1836 (R1869) (R1953) (R1960) (R1993) (R2002) (R2012)
Truss Type: Unique combination of Multiple Kingpost, Queenpost and Arches
Dimensions: 2 Span, 191 Feet

Photo Tips: From the west side there are excellent panoramic views from both sides which can include the dam
Notes: This is Vermont's third oldest bridge and has a unique and interesting construction. In 2011 it was damaged by Hurricane Irene and in 2012 was undergoing repairs

World Index Number: VT/45-14-12
National Register of Historic Places: August 28, 1973

Lincoln Covered Bridge
County: Windsor, Vermont
Township: Woodstock

GPS Position: N 43° 36.009' W 72° 34.139'
Directions: From the town of West Woodstock take US-4 southwest for 0.3 miles where you find the bridge
Crosses: Ottauquechee River
Carries: Fletcher Hill Road

Builder: R.W. & B.H. Pinney
Year Built: 1877
Truss Type: Pratt Truss with Arch
Dimensions: 1 Span, 136 Feet

Photo Tips: Open easy views from all sides
Notes: The Pratt Truss with an arch is an interesting combination, perhaps unique to this bridge

World Index Number: VT/45-14-13
National Register of Historic Places: August 28, 1973

Middle Covered Bridge
County: Windsor, Vermont
Township: Woodstock

GPS Position: N 43° 37.483' W 72° 31.233'
Directions: From the Village of Woodstock turn north on Union St off of US-4
Crosses: Ottauquechee River
Carries: Union St

Builder: Milton S. Graton
Year Built: 1969 (R1976) (R1989)
Truss Type: Town
Dimensions: 1 Span, 139 Feet

Photo Tips: Portal views are easy but watch for traffic. No easy side views are available
Notes: Found in the middle of the village, it has a pedestrian walkway as well as a lane for vehicles. It was arsoned in 1974 but the bridge was saved and repaired. Some of the arsonists had their wages seized to cover the repairs

World Index Number: VT/45-14-15
National Register of Historic Places: Not listed

South Pomfret Covered Bridge (Teago)
County: Windsor, Vermont
Township: Pomfret

GPS Position: N 43° 39.732' W 72° 32.193'
Directions: From the village of South Pomfret, go east on Pomfret Road for about 0.2 miles
Crosses: Barnard Brook
Carries: Farm lane

Builder: Not known
Year Built: 1870 (M1973)
Truss Type: Town
Dimensions: 1 Span, 39 Feet

Photo Tips: It is on private property but can be photographed with a longer lens
Notes: This bridge is half of an original bridge known as the Garfield Bridge located in Hyde Park in Lamoille County. It was spilt and moved to two locations by a developer. The other bridge, Twigg-Smith Covered Bridge, collapsed in 2002

World Index Number: VT/45-14-18
National Register of Historic Places: Not listed

North Hartland West Twin Covered Bridge
County: Windsor, Vermont
Township: Hartland

GPS Position: N 43° 35.611' W 72° 20.973'
Directions: From the town of North Hartland take Ewarts Drts Drive south off US-5 and take the first left on Mill St. The bridge is then a short distance
Crosses: Ottauquechee River
Carries: Mill St.
Builder: Not Known
Year Built: 2001
Truss Type: Town
Dimensions: 1 Span, 81 Feet

Photo Tips: It is easy to get a shot with both bridges in the frame. Side views are available with care
Notes: The first bridge on this site was built in about 1872 and was destroyed in a hurricane in 1938. This bridge is an authentic replica completed in 2001 Just east of this bridge is another called the Williard Covered Bridge

World Index Number: VT/45-14-64#2
National Register of Historic Places: Not listed

Windsor-Cornish Covered Bridge
County: Windsor, VT and Sullivan, NH
Township: Windsor, VT and Cornish, NH

GPS Position: N 43° 28.375' W 72° 22.996'
Directions: From Windsor, VT take US-5/ VT-12/ Main St. south for 0.3 mi and turn left on Bridge St. From Cornish, NH take Mill Village Rd and continue on Town House/NH12 for 1.5 miles and the bridge will appear on your left
Crosses: Connecticut River
Carries: Bridge Street, VT amd Cornish Toll Road, NH
Builder: James Tasker & Bela J. Fletcher
Year Built: 1866 (R1887) (R1892)(R1887) (R1925) (R1887) (R1938) (R1955) (R1977) (R1989) (R2001)
Truss Type: Town
Dimensions: 2 Span, 449 Feet, 2 Lanes
Photo Tips: There are good views from front and sides but watch for traffic
Notes: This is one of the finest covered bridges in North America with a toe in Vermont and the bulk in New Hampshire. It is the longest two span bridge in the world

World Index Number: 38-33-03
National Register of Historic Places: Not listed

Tours

The following self guided tours provide an efficient order to visit groups of bridges in various counties.

Addison County Tour (4 Bridges) (1 hour driving)

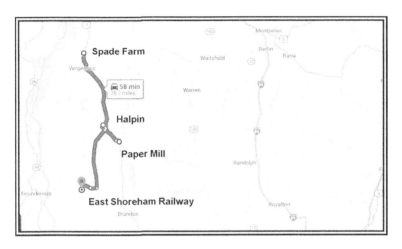

Spade Farm Covered Bridge	N 44° 12.415' W 73° 14.885'
Halpin Covered Bridge	N 44° 03.002' W 73° 08.459'
Pulp Mill Covered Bridge	N 44° 01.453' W 73° 10.663'
East Shoreham Railway Bridge	N 43° 51.561' W 73° 15.363'

Bennington County Tour (5 Bridges) (45 minutes driving)

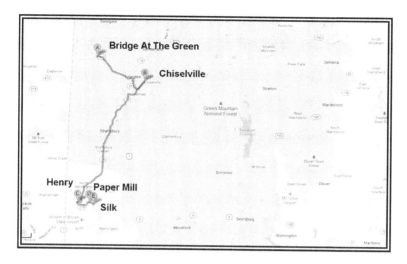

Bridge At The Green CB	N 43° 06.272' W 73° 13.208'
Chiselville Covered Bridge	N 43° 04.345' W 73° 07.959'
Henry Covered Bridge	N 42° 54.737' W 73° 15.288'
Paper Mill Covered Bridge	N 42° 54.737' W 73° 15.288'
Silk Covered Bridge	N 42° 54.577' W 73° 13.519'

Caledonia County Tour (5 Bridges) (40 minutes driving)

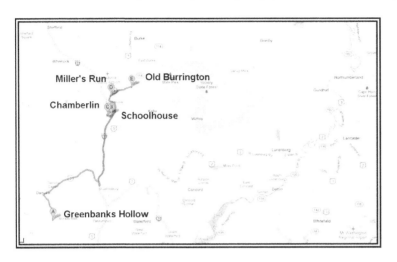

Greenbanks Hollow CB	N 44° 22.644' W 72° 07.328'
Schoolhouse Covered Bridge	N 44° 30.977' W 72° 00.591'
Chamberlin Mill CB	N 44° 30.963' W 72° 00.876'
Miller's Run Covered Bridge	N 44° 32.533' W 72° 00.596'
Old Burrington CB	N 44° 33.198' W 71° 58.165'

Chittenden County Tour (5 Bridges) (1.5 hours driving)

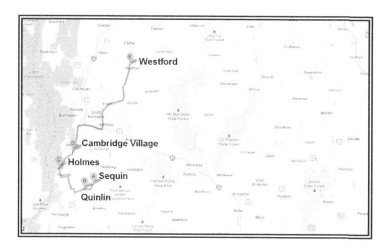

Sequin Covered Bridge	N 44° 17.333' W 73° 09.002'
Quinlin Covered Bridge	N 44° 16.559' W 73° 11.047'
Holmes Covered Bridge	N 44° 19.970' W 73° 16.940'
Cambridge Village CB	N 44° 22.397' W 73° 13.859'
Westford Covered Bridge	N 44° 36.748' W 73° 00.462'

Connecticut River Tour (3 Bridges) (1.75 hours driving)

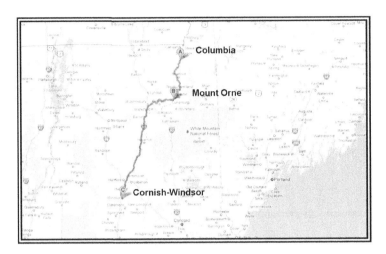

Columbia Covered Bridge	N 44° 51.159' W 71° 33.050'
Mount Orne Covered Bridge	N 44° 27.634' W 71° 39.206'
Cornish-Windsor CB	N 43° 28.375' W 72° 22.996'

Franklin County Tour (8 Bridges) (1.5 hours driving)

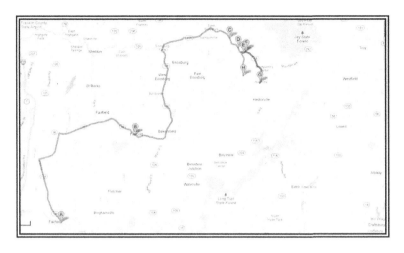

Maple Street Covered Bridge	N 44° 39.803' W 73° 00.630'
East Fairfield Covered Bridge	N 44° 47.168' W 72° 51.719'
Hopkins Covered Bridge	N 44° 55.229' W 72° 40.366'
Longley Covered Bridge	N 44° 54.438' W 72° 39.333'
Comstock Covered Bridge	N 44° 53.969' W 72° 38.669'
Fuller Covered Bridge	N 44° 54.199' W 72° 38.376'
Hutchins Covered Bridge	N 44° 51.520' W 72° 36.769'
West Hill Covered Bridge	N 44° 52.069' W 72° 38.868'

Lamoille County Tour (13 Bridges) (2.5 hours driving)

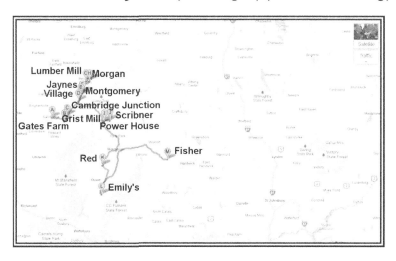

Gates Farm Covered Bridge	N 44° 38.741' W 72° 52.339'
Grist Mill Covered Bridge	N 43° 02.930' W 72° 41.789'
Cambridge Junction CB	N 44° 39.088' W 72° 48.798'
Village Covered Bridge	N 44° 39.088' W 72° 48.798'
Montgomery Covered Bridge	N 44° 42.348' W 72° 45.616'
Jaynes Covered Bridge	N 44° 42.719' W 72° 45.388'
Lumber Mill Covered Bridge	N 44° 44.636' W 72° 44.476'
Morgan Covered Bridge	N 44° 44.616' W 72° 43.684'
Power House Covered Bridge	N 44° 38.161' W 72° 40.198'
Scribner Covered Bridge	N 44° 38.383' W 72° 38.911'
Red Covered Bridge	N 44° 31.109' W 72° 40.669'
Emily's Covered Bridge	N 44° 26.422' W 72° 40.788'
Fisher Railroad Covered Bridge	N 44° 31.936' W 72° 25.660'

Orange County Tour (11 Bridges) (2 hours driving)

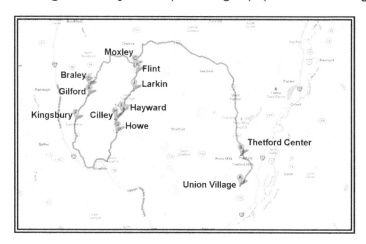

Union Village	N 43° 47.321' W 72° 15.223'
Thetford Center CB	N 43° 49.939' W 72° 15.149'
Moxley Covered Bridge	N 43° 57.436' W 72° 27.816'
Braley Covered Bridge	N 43° 55.704' W 72° 33.337'
Gilford Covered Bridge	N 43° 54.977' W 72° 33.330'
Kingsbury Covered Bridge	N 43° 52.850' W 72° 34.903'
Howe Covered Bridge	N 43° 51.890' W 72° 29.901'
Cilley Covered Bridge	N 43° 52.977' W 72° 30.256'
Hayward Covered Bridge	N 43° 53.485' W 72° 29.486'
Larkin Covered Bridge	N 43° 55.381' W 72° 27.894'
Flint Covered Bridge	N 43° 56.956' W 72° 27.495'

Rutland County Tour (7 Bridges) (1 hour driving)

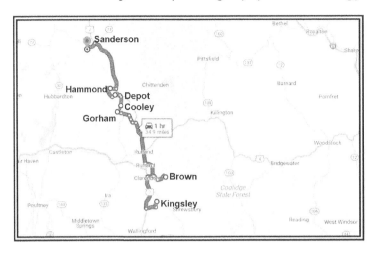

Kingsley Covered Bridge	N 43° 31.418' W 72° 56.459'
Brown Covered Bridge	N 43° 33.962' W 72° 55.107'
Gorham Covered Bridge	N 43° 40.798' W 73° 02.237'
Cooley Covered Bridge	N 43° 41.427' W 73° 01.691'
Depot Covered Bridge	N 43° 42.577' W 73° 02.557'
Hammond Covered Bridge	N 43° 43.238' W 73° 03.239'
Sanderson Covered Bridge	N 43° 47.367' W 73° 06.686'

Washington County Tour (12 Bridges) (3 Hours driving)

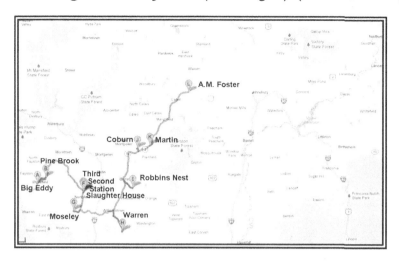

Big Eddy Covered Bridge	N 44° 11.362' W 72° 49.409'
Pine Brook Covered Bridge	N 44° 12.339' W 72° 47.549'
Third Covered Bridge	N 44° 10.425' W 72° 39.337'
Second Covered Bridge	N 44° 10.366' W 72° 39.151'
Station Covered Bridge	N 44° 10.351' W 72° 39.084'
Slaughter House CB	N 44° 10.112' W 72° 39.268'
Moseley Covered Bridge	N 44° 07.709' W 72° 41.775'
Warren Covered Bridge	N 44° 06.672' W 72° 51.411'
Robbins Nest CB	N 44° 10.735' W 72° 28.261'
Coburn Covered Bridge	N 44° 16.855' W 72° 27.233'
Martin Covered Bridge	N 44° 25.416' W 72° 16.042'
A.M. Foster Covered Bridge	N 44° 25.416' W 72° 16.042'

Windham County Tour (9 Bridges) (2 hours driving)

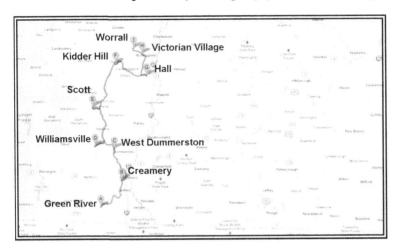

| Green River Covered Bridge | N 42° 46.531' W 72° 40.018' |
| West Dummerston CB | N 42° 56.170' W 72° 36.777' |

Green River Covered Bridge — N 42° 46.531' W 72° 40.018'
Creamery Covered CB — N 42° 51.012' W 72° 35.119'
West Dummerston CB — N 42° 56.170' W 72° 36.777'
Williamsville Covered Bridge — N 42° 56.653' W 72° 44.306'
Scott Covered Bridge — N 43° 02.930' W 72° 41.789'
Kidder Hill Covered Bridge — N 43° 10.119' W 72° 36.333'
Hall Covered Bridge — N 43° 08.210' W 72° 29.267'
Victorian Village CB — N 43° 11.680' W 72° 30.079'
Worrall Covered Bridge — N 43° 12.702' W 72° 32.127'

Windsor County Tour (13 Bridges) (2.5 hours driving)

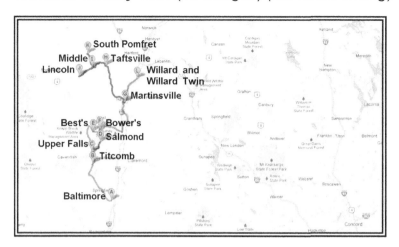

Baltimore Covered Bridge	N 43° 16.240' W 72° 26.877'
Titcomb Covered Bridge	N 43° 22.131' W 72° 31.056'
Upper Falls Covered Bridge	N 43° 23.893' W 72° 31.337'
Salmond Covered Bridge	N 43° 25.626' W 72° 29.285'
Best's Covered Bridge	N 43° 27.300' W 72° 30.986'
Bower's Covered Bridge	N 43° 27.662' W 72° 29.438'
Martinsville Covered Bridge	N 43° 31.955' W 72° 23.749'
Taftsville Covered Bridge	N 43° 37.866' W 72° 28.058'
Middle Covered Bridge	N 43° 37.483' W 72° 31.233'
Lincoln Covered Bridge	N 43° 36.009' W 72° 34.139'
South Pomfret CB	N 43° 39.732' W 72° 32.193'
Willard Covered Bridge	N 43° 35.611' W 72° 20.973'
Willard Twin Covered Bridge	N 43° 35.611' W 72° 20.973'

Recently Lost

Twin Covered Bridge

Maine
Watson Settlement Covered Bridge
ME/19-02-01x, 1911, Howe, 2 spans 112 feet
Destroyed by fire on July 19, 2021

Vermont
Hectorville Covered Bridge
VT/45-06-06x, 1883, Town and King, 1 span 54 feet
In Storage since 2002

Salisbury Station Covered Bridge
VT/45-01-01x, 1865, Town, 1 span 155 feet
Destroyed by fire September 10, 2016

River Road Covered Bridge
VT/45-10-03x, 1910, Town, 1 span 93 feet
Lost to fire on February 6, 2021

Twin Covered Bridge
VT/45-11-10#2x, 1850, Town, 1 span 64 feet
Used as storage shed

Glossary

Abutment: The abutments are the bridge supports on each side bank. Usually they were originally constructed of stone but they have often been replaced or supplemented with concrete through the years.

Arch: A curved timber or timber set which is shaped in a curve and functions as a support of the bridge.

Bed timbers: Timbers between the abutment and the truss or bottom chord.

Brace or bracing: A diagonal timber or timber set used to support the trusses.

Bridge Deck: The roadway through the bridge.

Buttress: Wood or metal members on the exterior sides which connect the floor beams and the top of the truss. Used to keep the bridge structure from twisting under wind, water and snow loads.

Camber: A planned curve in the structure to compensate for the weight of the structure.

Chord: The horizontal members extending the length of the truss meant to carry the load
to the abutments.

Dead load: The load of the weight of the bridge itself.

Deck: The pathway through the bridge used by pedestrians or vehicles.

Pier: Stone/concrete supports built in the stream bed to support the bridge

Portal: The bridge's entrances.

Post: The truss's vertical members.

Span: The bridge length measured between the abutments.

Treenails or trunnels: Pins or dowels turned from hardwood, driven into holes drilled into the members of the truss to hold them together. Also used in mortised joints.

Truss: The framework which carries the load of the bridge and distributes it to the abutments.

Truss Types

A Truss is a system of ties and struts which are connected to act like a single beam to distribute and carry a load. In covered bridges, these Trusses carry the load to stone abutments at each side and perhaps piers in between. Following are the most common types of Trusses used in Covered Bridges.

Brown

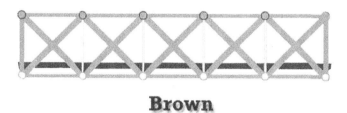

Brown

Josiah Brown Jr., of Buffalo, New York, patented this system in 1857.It consists of diagonal cross compression members connected to horizontal top and bottom stringers and is known for economic use of materials. It was only used in Michigan where there are a couple of surviving members.

Burr Arch

Burr Arch

Invented in 1804 by Theodore Burr, the Burr Arch is one of the most commonly found structures in Covered Bridge design. It is often used in combination with multiple kingposts. The ends of the arch are buried in the abutments

Childs

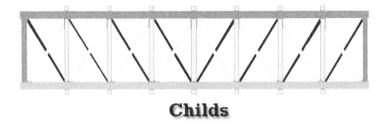

Childs

The Childs Truss System is essentially a multiple kingpost with half of the diagonal timbers replaced with iron bars.

Howe

Howe Truss

The Howe Truss was patented in 1840 by William Howe. It involves the use of vertical metal rods between the joints of wooden diagonals.

Kingpost

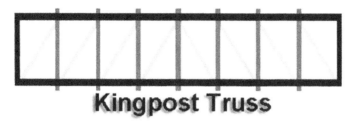

Kingpost Truss

Kingpost is the simplest form of Truss with two diagonal members on a bottom chord, often with a vertical post connecting to the diagonals. The multiple Kingpost involves a series of Kingposts symmetrical from the bridges center.

Long

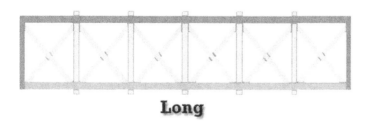

Long

The Long Truss was patented by Stephen Long in 1830. It is a series of X shaped diagonals connected to vertical posts.

Paddleford

Paddleford

Peter Paddleford worked with the Long Truss system and eventually adapted it with a system of interlocking braces. he was never able to patent the system due to challenges from the owners of the Long Truss patent. However there are a number of New Hampshire and Vermont bridges which use the Paddleford system

Partridge

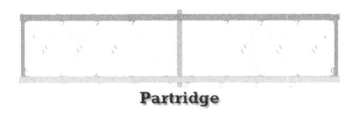

Partridge

Reuben L. Partridge received a patent for a design similar to the Smith system but adding terminal braces at the end and a central vertical member.

Pratt

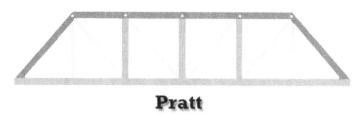

Pratt

The Pratt truss was patented in 1844 by Caleb Pratt and his son Thomas Willis Pratt. The design uses vertical members for compression and horizontal members to respond to tension.

Queenpost

Queenpost Truss

The Queenpost has the peak of the kingpost type replaced with a horizontal top chord which allows for a longer span.

Smith

Smith Truss

Robert W. Smith received patents in 1867 and 1869 for variations of his system.

Town

Town Truss

The Town or lattice system was patented by Ithiel Town in 1820. It involved a system of overlapping diagonals in a lattice pattern connected at the intersection by Tree nails or trunnels, wooden pegs or dowels. It had the advantages in that it could be constructed by unskilled labor and local materials could be used.

Warren

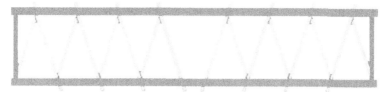

Warren

Patented in 1848 by two Englishmen, one of whom was named James Warren, it consists of parallel upper and lower chords with diagonal connecting members forming a series of equilateral triangles.

References

National Society for the Preservation of Covered Bridges
http://www.coveredbridgesociety.org

New York State Covered Bridge Society
http://www.nycoveredbridges.org

Vermont Covered Bridge Society
http://www.vermontbridges.com/

Covered Bridge Society of Oregon
http://www.covered-bridges.org/

The Theodore Burr Covered Bridge Society of Pennsylvania
http://www.tbcbspa.com/

Indiana Covered Bridge Society
http://www.indianacrossings.org/

Ohio Historic Bridge Association
http://oldohiobridges.com/ohba/index.htm

Harold Stiver Image Gallery
https://haroldstiver.smugmug.com/Galleries/Themes/Covered-Bridges

Photography Credits

Gianina Lindsey CC Flickr: Tannery Hill Covered Bridge, New Hampshire

All other photographs are the work of the author

Other Books by Harold Stiver

Unless noted, there are Print and eBook editions available for the following.

Birding Guide to Orkney
Guide to Photographing Birds
Ontario Lighthouses
Ontario's Old Mills
Ontario Waterfalls

Alabama Covered Bridges (eBook)
California Covered Bridges (eBook)
Connecticut Covered Bridges (eBook)
Georgia Covered Bridges (eBook)
Indiana Covered Bridges
Maine Covered Bridges (eBook)
Maryland Covered Bridges (eBook)
Massachusetts Covered Bridges (eBook)
Michigan Covered Bridges (eBook)
New England Covered Bridges
Covered Bridges of the Mid-Atlantic
Covered Bridges of the South
New Brunswick Covered Bridges
New Hampshire Covered Bridges
New York Covered Bridges
Ohio's Covered Bridges
Oregon Covered Bridges
The Covered Bridges of Kentucky (eBook)
The Covered Bridges of Kentucky and Tennessee
The Covered Bridges of Tennessee (eBook)
Vermont's Covered Bridges
The Covered Bridges of Virginia (eBook)
The Covered Bridges of Virginia and West Virginia
The Covered Bridges of West Virginia (eBook)
Washington Covered Bridges (eBook)
West Coast Covered Bridges

Index

Connecticut

Maine

Massachusetts

Groveton Covered Bridge	71
Happy Corner Covered Bridge	68
Honeymoon Covered Bridge	53
Jack O'Lantern Resort Covered Bridge	86
Jackson Covered Bridge	53
Joppa Road Covered Bridge	95
Keniston Covered Bridge	92
Livermore Covered Bridge	90
McDermott Covered Bridge	107
Mechanic Street Covered Bridge	72
Meriden Covered Bridge	109
Mill Covered Bridge	109
Mount Orne Covered Bridge	76
New England College Covered Bridge	99
Old Russell Hill Rdc Covered Bridge	90
Packard Hill Covered Bridge	87
Pier Railroad Covered Bridge	104
Pinsley Railroad Covered Bridge	85
Pittsburg Covered Bridge	70
Prentiss Covered Bridge	108
River Road Covered Bridge	69
Rollins Farm Covered Bridge	101
Rowell Covered Bridge	97
Saco River Covered Bridge	55
Sawyer's Crossing Covered Bridge	65
Slate Covered Bridge	66
Smith Millennium Covered Bridge	83
Snyder Brook Covered Bridge	74
Squam River Covered Bridge	88
Stark Covered Bridge	72
Stony Morrell Covered Bridge	61
Sulphite Railroad Covered Bridge	98
Swift River Covered Bridge	56
Swiftwater Covered Bridge	77
Tannery Hill Covered Bridge	52
Thompson Covered Bridge	64
Upper Village Covered Bridge	62
Wason Pond Covered Bridge	100
Waterloo Station Covered Bridge	94
Wentworth County Club Covered Bridge	60

Coddling Hollow Covered Bridge	160
Columbia Covered Bridge	139
Comstock Covered Bridge	144
Cooley Covered Bridge	180
Coventry Covered Bridge	174
Cox Brook Covered Bridge	187
Creamery CB, Franklin County	148
Creamery CB, Windham County	194
DeGosh Covered Bridge	155
Depot CB, Rutland County	179
Depot CB, Windham County	203
Downer's Covered Bridge	209
East Fairfield Covered Bridge	143
East Shoreham Railroad CB	122
Emily's Covered Bridge	157
Fisher Railroad Covered Bridge	161
Flint Covered Bridge	171
Fuller Covered Bridge	145
Gates Farm Covered Bridge	151
Gilford Covered Bridge	164
Gold Brook Covered Bridge	157
Goodnough Covered Bridge	177
Gorham Covered Bridge	177
Great Eddy Covered Bridge	190
Green River Covered Bridge	197
Greenbanks Hollow Covered Bridge	128
Grist Mill Covered Bridge	149
Guy Covered Bridge	162
Hall Covered Bridge	199
Halpin Covered Bridge	120
Hammond Covered Bridge	178
Harnois Covered Bridge	147
Hayward Covered Bridge	170
Head Covered Bridge	147
Henry Covered Bridge	124
High Covered Bridge	120
Hollow Covered Bridge	181
Holmes Covered Bridge	134
Hopkins Covered Bridge	141

Station CB, Washington County	185
Sterling Brook Covered Bridge	156
Stony Brook Covered Bridge	184
Stoughton Covered Bridge	207
Stowe Hollow Covered Bridge	157
Swallows Covered Bridge	210
Taftsville Covered Bridge	212
Teago Covered Bridge	215
Thetford Center Covered Bridge	165
Third Covered Bridge	188
Titcomb Covered Bridge	207
Union Village Covered Bridge	166
Upper CB, Belvidere Township	153
Upper CB, Chittenden County	135
Upper CB, Orange County	165
Upper CB, Waterville Township	160
Upper Cox Brook Covered Bridge	188
Upper Falls Covered Bridge	209
Victorian Village Covered Bridge	203
Village CB, Franklin County	142
Village CB, Lamoille County	158
Village CB, Washington County	190
Warren Covered Bridge	191
West Dummerston Covered Bridge	195
West Hill Covered Bridge	148
Westford Covered Bridge	137
Whitcomb Covered Bridge	130
Wilder Covered Bridge	189
Willard Covered Bridge	205
Williamsville Covered Bridge	198
Windsor-Cornish Covered Bridge	217
Worrall Covered Bridge	200

Made in United States
North Haven, CT
29 November 2024

61172613R00137